WORKBOOK

FIRE & REIGN

By Jerry Sheveland

A 10-week journey into spiritual renewal

Harvest Publications
© 2005 by Baptist General Conference
Cover and text design: Sharon Nelsen

ISBN: 0-935797-75-0

For more information, contact:
  President's Office
  Baptist General Conference
  2002 S. Arlington Heights Road
  Arlington Heights, IL 60005-4193
  800-323-4215
  www.bgcworld.org

CONTENTS

Again the answer is, probably not. Your church is made up of a group of people God has called together. God may move in power and do wonderful things in your midst, but these would call attention to Christ's glory, not your giftedness. More likely they would be along these lines:

- Drawing people to repentance before a Holy God who hates every form and expression of sin.
- Reawakening believers to Christ's priorities for his church.
- Strengthening core convictions and practices that bring glory to God and the gospel to unbelievers worldwide.
- Empowering disciples to make a measurable impact for Christ on the community in which your church ministers — resulting in less sin and more holiness.
- Stirring a passion to know Jesus, become more like him and display him to a world that needs him.
- Prompting people to reconcile long-held differences, seek each other's gain and love one another as Christ loves his church.

So, do you want more of the Holy Spirit's power and presence in your life and in your church? Do you want the Spirit to expand Christ's reign in you, your church, your community, our nation and the world? Do you desire the purifying fire of God's Spirit for the reign of God's Son?

If so, then you've come to the right place. This 10-week study will take you deep into the Book of Acts in order to draw you back to Christ's priorities for his church. We'll study the first seven chapters of Acts to see how God raised up a spiritually empowered congregation — the Jerusalem church — capable of touching all nations. It's a model for any church.

Each weekend your pastor will bring a message on the key theme of the week. Then five days a week you'll work through 15-minute lessons in this workbook. This leads to a small group experience, where you'll reflect and discuss what the Lord is teaching about the Holy Spirit and his work. And you'll be invited to fast and pray on the first Tuesday of each month, for the reign of Jesus in your life, your church and your community. Your church may also host a special renewal weekend with a guest speaker.

Let me conclude with a few words about the author. I've known Jerry Sheveland for more than 25 years. For 2 1/2 years I sat in his first church three times a week, enrapt by his strong expository preaching. I've watched his career as he pastored three other strong churches of various sizes. As president of the Baptist General Conference, he has proven himself a man of resolute integrity, with strong leadership skills, remarkable insight into church dynamics and a genuine dependence upon Spirit-empowered ministry. He is an apt and able guide for our journey through Acts 1-7.

It's high time we gave Christ's Spirit more authority in our lives and in our churches. *Fire & Reign* is a rock-solid, no-nonsense first leg of that journey. Having worked through the manuscript several times, and watched numerous takes and retakes of the DVD segments, I confidently recommend this study to you and your church — without reservation. May the fire of God's Spirit expand the reign of God's Son as you join others in this journey into spiritual renewal.

Bob Putman, editor

Lesson One

Embracing Christ's Mission

In my former book, Theophilus, I wrote about all that Jesus began to do and to teach ²until the day he was taken up to heaven, after giving instructions through the Holy Spirit to the apostles he had chosen. ³After his suffering, he showed himself to these men and gave many convincing proofs that he was alive. He appeared to them over a period of forty days and spoke about the kingdom of God. ⁴On one occasion, while he was eating with them, he gave them this command: "Do not leave Jerusalem, but wait for the gift my Father promised, which you have heard me speak about. ⁵For John baptized with water, but in a few days you will be baptized with the Holy Spirit."

⁶So when they met together, they asked him, "Lord, are you at this time going to restore the kingdom to Israel?"

⁷He said to them: "It is not for you to know the times or dates the Father has set by his own authority. ⁸But you will receive power when the Holy Spirit comes on you; and you will be my witnesses in Jerusalem, and in all Judea and Samaria, and to the ends of the earth."

⁹After he said this, he was taken up before their very eyes, and a cloud hid him from their sight.

¹⁰They were looking intently up into the sky as he was going, when suddenly two men dressed in white stood beside them. ¹¹"Men of Galilee," they said, "why do you stand here looking into the sky? This same Jesus, who has been taken from you into heaven, will come back in the same way you have seen him go into heaven."

Acts 1:1-11

25"All this I have spoken while still with you. 26But the Counselor, the Holy Spirit, whom the Father will send in my name, will teach you all things and will remind you of everything I have said to you."
— John 14:25-26

Jesus is at work **through his Word**. *"...he was taken up to heaven, after giving instructions...."* He continues to teach his followers by means of his instruction, the Bible. Jesus fulfilled all the Law and prophets contained in the Old Testament, and he delivered the New Testament through his prophets and apostles. ***What did Jesus promise his apostles in John 14:25-26?*** _____

_____

_____

_____

_____

_____

5"Now I am going to him who sent me, yet none of you asks me, 'Where are you going?' 6Because I have said these things, you are filled with grief. 7But I tell you the truth: It is for your good that I am going away. Unless I go away, the Counselor will not come to you; but if I go, I will send him to you."
— John 16:5-7

Jesus is at work **through his Spirit**. *"...he was taken up to heaven, after giving instructions through the Holy Spirit...."* Jesus not only gave us his instructions, his Word — he also gave us his Holy Spirit. Jesus explained to his followers that it was better for them to have him ascend to heaven. By sending his Spirit, Jesus could be everywhere present among his followers. ***How did Jesus explain this truth in John 16:5-7?*** _____

_____

_____

_____

_____

_____

19Consequently, you are no longer foreigners and aliens, but fellow citizens with God's people and members of God's household, 20built on the foundation of the apostles and prophets, with Christ Jesus himself as the chief cornerstone. 21In him the whole building is joined together and rises to become a holy temple in the Lord. 22And in him you too are being built together to become a dwelling in which God lives by his Spirit.
— Ephesians 2:19-22

Jesus is at work **through his people**. *"...he was taken up to heaven, after giving instructions through the Holy Spirit to the apostles he had chosen."* Jesus chose and commissioned his apostles to raise up his church — his people among the nations of this earth. The Apostle Paul would later write about this truth in Ephesians 2:19-22. ***What did Paul teach about the foundation of the church?*** _____

_____

_____

_____

_____

_____

_____

_____

_____

When Jesus affirmed Peter's chosen role as an apostle, the Lord made it clear that he himself would accomplish the mission. He said, *"…I will build my church"* (Matt. 16:18). Like Peter, we now have our part to play. And like Peter, we must embrace the truth that this is Christ's mission, and he is the one who will build his church around the world. ***Take a moment to write a brief prayer asking the Lord Jesus to show you your part in his mission.***_____

_____

_____

_____

_____

Day Two

It's Christ's kingdom mission — he is restoring God's reign in the lives of his followers

Jesus appeared to his disciples for 40 days between his resurrection and ascension. What did he teach them over that six-week period of time? Luke gives us the answer.

> *He appeared to them over a period of forty days and spoke about the kingdom of God* (Acts 1:3).

The kingdom of God was Jesus' frequent theme over the years he spent discipling his followers. The four Gospels record Jesus speaking about the kingdom of God some 80 times. The people of Israel had been waiting centuries for the Messiah, an heir of King David, to restore God's wise, just and loving reign to his people. It is no wonder that the disciples asked Jesus, *"Lord, are you at this time going to restore the kingdom to Israel?"* (Acts 1:6). It was the longing of their hearts to see rebellious lives and false kingdoms bow before God's anointed one. They wanted the Lord to get the worship, love and obedience that is worthy of his glory.

Jesus responded to their kingdom questions with these words, *"It is not for you to know the times or dates the Father has set by his own authority"* (Acts 1:7). What was he saying? He was affirming that a day would come when he would indeed restore God's kingdom to Israel. He would claim his rightful throne. All the Old Testament promises about the Messiah would be fulfilled. The timing of that coming day, however, was the Father's business, not theirs.

So what is Christ's kingdom mission today as we wait for his return? The heart of his mission is not to fill churches with religious people or even to bring unbelievers to a profession of faith. The heart of his mission is to restore God's reign in the lives of his followers. Matthew recorded Christ's mission statement with these words:

> Then Jesus came to them and said, "All authority in heaven and on earth has been given to me. Therefore go and make disciples of all nations, baptizing them in the name of the Father and of the Son and of the Holy Spirit, and teaching them to obey everything I have commanded you. And surely I am with you always, to the very end of the age. (Matt. 28:18-20).

Making disciples among all nations is about exalting Christ's supreme authority in heaven and on earth. And it is about multiplying baptized followers who learn to obey his commands and enjoy his presence. In short, it is about his kingdom.

The Apostle Paul used three "R" words to describe how the Lord brings us into his kingdom: "rescued," "redemption" and "reconciled." *Study Colossians 1:12-14 and 1:21-23. Then explain those three words in relation to Christ's kingdom:*

Rescued (verse 13) _____

_____

_____

Redemption (verse 14) _____

_____

_____

Reconciled (verses 21-23) _____

_____

_____

Christ died on the cross and rose from the dead so that people around the world might be rescued from a kingdom of darkness and death, and as forgiven people be reconciled to God and his kingdom of light. Think about how Jesus taught his disciples to pray, *"Our Father in heaven, hallowed be your name, your kingdom come, your will be done on earth as it is in heaven…"* (Matt. 6:9-10). Consider how he called his followers to *"…seek first his kingdom and his righteousness…"* (Matt. 6:33). *Then ask yourself, "How am I seeking the reign of Christ in my life and the lives of others?"* _____

_____

_____

_____

A few months ago I visited missionaries Rick and Carol Stark, who minister in Pé Pequena, a hilltop slum community within the larger metroplex of Rio de Janeiro, Brazil. It is a dangerous and impoverished part of the city largely controlled by gangs and drug lords. Rick and Carol serve alongside a Brazilian pastor and a small group of

12giving thanks to the Father, who has qualified you to share in the inheritance of the saints in the kingdom of light. 13For he has rescued us from the dominion of darkness and brought us into the kingdom of the Son he loves, 14in whom we have redemption, the forgiveness of sins.
— **Colossians 1:12-14**

21Once you were alienated from God and were enemies in your minds because of your evil behavior. 22But now he has reconciled you by Christ's physical body through death to present you holy in his sight, without blemish and free from accusation— 23if you continue in your faith, established and firm, not moved from the hope held out in the gospel. This is the gospel that you heard and that has been proclaimed to every creature under heaven, and of which I, Paul, have become a servant.
— **Colossians 1:21-23**

Christians who are committed to bringing the influence of Christ's reign into that poor and violent place. I watched them minister together to street kids and reach out to young people and their parents. Out of loving ministry a new church named Boa Vista (Good View) is being born. A circle of disciples is bearing witness through shared ministry, worship and fellowship to the living presence of King Jesus. One more stronghold of darkness is being invaded by the kingdom of light.

Day Three

It's Christ's global mission — he is reproducing his church among all nations

But you will receive power when the Holy Spirit comes on you; and you will be my witnesses in Jerusalem, and in all Judea and Samaria, and to the ends of the earth (Acts 1:8).

We watch the global nature of Christ's mission unfold as we turn the pages of the Book of Acts. In the first seven chapters we see the church established among the Jews in Jerusalem. The next three chapters document how the gospel spread into the wider sphere of Judea and Samaria, beginning to reach Samaritans and Gentiles as well as Jews. Then starting with the story of the Antioch church in chapter 11, we witness the expansion of the church to the ends of the earth.

It should not surprise us that Christ desires to extend his kingdom reign and raise up his church among every group of people in the world. Yet too often our circle of concern is largely confined to the places where we live, work and worship. Missionary author Don Richardson made a statement that I will never forget. He said, "We like to think that the Book of Acts is the story of the church bringing the gospel to the world. In fact, it is the story of God's Spirit overcoming the reluctance of the church to bring the gospel to the world." I think Don Richardson was right. It took persecution to move the Jerusalem church into the surrounding world to reach Gentiles as well as Jews. May Christ give our churches a more ready willingness to embrace his mission.

It is popular to use the *"…Jerusalem, Judea and Samaria and to the ends of the earth…"* language to describe a mission that begins at home and then extends to ever-wider circles of geography. We must, however, recognize that Jerusalem was not home for most of the early disciples. They were from Galilee to the north. Christ commanded them to remain in Jerusalem and not return home. Why? The church was launched in Jerusalem for strategic and symbolic reasons. Strategically it was a large city populated by Jewish people awaiting the Messiah and who witnessed Christ's death and resurrection. Thousands were responsive to the gospel, and the church grew in size and strength. Jerusalem was a strategic place to launch a global movement.

More important, Jerusalem stood as the symbolic center of God's plan to bring redemption to the nations, beginning with his chosen people, Israel. Jerusalem is the place the promised Messiah will reign. It is the place of Christ's return. Peter spoke to his Jewish listeners in Jerusalem and explained it like this:

> And you are heirs of the prophets and of the covenant God made with your fathers. He said to Abraham, "Through your offspring all peoples on earth will be blessed." When God raised up his servant, he sent him first to you to bless you by turning each of you from your wicked ways (Acts 3:25-26).

Out of love for his Father and compassion for lost, needy people, Christ raised up his church in the symbolic center of his kingdom and then reproduced his church from Jerusalem to communities in Judea, Samaria and beyond. If we embrace his mission, we embrace his passion for people of the world wherever they live.

How does Christ's return relate to the global nature of his mission? Read Matthew 24:14.

_____

_____

_____

_____

How will people from every nation worship Christ when his mission is complete? Describe the scene John records in Revelation 7:9-10. _____

_____

_____

_____

Picture the 11 apostles listening to Jesus' global vision. Do you think they might have felt overwhelmed by the scope of his mission? Now think about your life and the other believers who make up your church. Think about the world you are called to reach. *How is God bringing people from other nations into the community where you live? How is the Lord already connecting your church with ministries in other parts of the world?*

_____

_____

_____

How do you think Jesus wants to expand your vision and the vision of your church for greater involvement in reaching the nations? _____

_____

_____

_____

14And this gospel of the kingdom will be preached in the whole world as a testimony to all nations, and then the end will come.

— **Matthew 24:14**

9After this I looked and there before me was a great multitude that no one could count, from every nation, tribe, people and language, standing before the throne and in front of the Lamb. They were wearing white robes and were holding palm branches in their hands. **10**And they cried out in a loud voice:

"Salvation belongs to our God, who sits on the throne, and to the Lamb."

— **Revelation 7:9-10**

Day Four

It's our mission too — Christ is revealing himself through Spirit-empowered witnesses

I was scheduled to preach at Heartland Church in Indianapolis, Ind., a church plant that was less than two years old. The congregation had already grown to more than 400 worshipers, and most of them were brand-new followers of Christ. The Saturday evening before I preached, pastor Darryn Scheske and one of his lay leaders took me out for dinner. Darryn explained that he wanted to talk to me before I stepped into the Sunday service the next morning. He wanted me to know in advance that this church plant was a work of God. He said, "Six months after attempting to start this church I gave up in discouragement. I told the Lord that if he wanted a new church in Indianapolis, he would have to build it." The young pastor went on to describe to me one experience after another of watching Christ work. Pastor Scheske worked hard, but it was Christ who built his church.

I was moved by the humility and faith I saw written across the face of that church planter. He is the kind of disciple Christ loves to use to accomplish his mission. It is what he longs to do in each of us: empower us with his Spirit so that we might bear witness to his living, reigning presence everywhere he sends us. Consider his promises to those first disciples:

> Do not leave Jerusalem, but wait for the gift my Father promised, which you have heard me speaking about. For John baptized with water, but in a few days you will be baptized with the Holy Spirit (Acts 1:4-5).

> But you will receive power when the Holy Spirit comes to you; and you will be my witnesses in Jerusalem, and in all Judea and Samaria, and to the ends of the earth (Acts 1:8).

We know that Christ fulfilled those promises in the lives of his apostles, but can he do it in us? Does he truly want to give us the power of his Holy Spirit so that our faith might be contagious and our witness effective?

When the Holy Spirit came upon the Jerusalem church, who received the power of the Spirit? Read Acts 2:1-4. _____

_____

_____

_____

_____

[1]When the day of Pentecost came, they were all together in one place. [2]Suddenly a sound like the blowing of a violent wind came from heaven and filled the whole house where they were sitting. [3]They saw what seemed to be tongues of fire that separated and came to rest on each of them. [4]All of them were filled with the Holy Spirit and began to speak in other tongues as the Spirit enabled them.

— Acts 2:1-4

17"In the last days," God says,"I will pour out my Spirit on all people. Your sons and daughters will prophesy, your young men will see visions, your old men will dream dreams."
— **Acts 2:17**

38Peter replied, "Repent and be baptized, every one of you, in the name of Jesus Christ for the forgiveness of your sins. And you will receive the gift of the Holy Spirit. 39The promise is for you and your children and for all who are far off—for all whom the Lord our God will call."
— **Acts 2:38-39**

When Peter explained the coming of the Holy Spirit, who did he say could receive the Spirit? See Acts 2:17 and Acts 2:38-39. _____

_____

_____

_____

_____

At the heart of our study in Acts is the conviction that Christ empowers his church to share his mission. Each of us as members of his church has our place in what Christ is doing and are given his Spirit to fulfill our part of the church's witness. As we worship, fellowship and minister together, Christ desires to display his kingdom in and among us. As we live and minister in the power of his Spirit, the more visible Christ becomes to the community that surrounds us.

Our tendency is to read this passage in Acts in an individual way so that it is about "me" being a witness in the power of the Spirit. Although that is true, there is a larger issue at stake. It is the issue of "our" being filled with his Spirit so that "we" as a church might display Christ's life and boldly witness to his gospel.

Christ's strategy is seen throughout the Book of Acts. Beginning in Jerusalem, Christ raised up a movement of Spirit-empowered churches capable of reproducing his life in disciples, leaders and congregations. Where the Holy Spirit is working in power, the life of Christ cannot be contained. It will reproduce from one life to another and one congregation to another until the world is filled with his witnesses.

How is the Holy Spirit at work in your life displaying Christ's love and truth to others?

_____

_____

_____

How is the Spirit working through the members of your church — young and old, women and men — to bring Christ's love and truth to people who live in your community?

_____

_____

_____

_____

Day Five

Until he comes…

After he said this, he was taken up before their very eyes, and a cloud hid him from their sight. They were looking intently up into the sky as he was going, when suddenly two men dressed in white stood beside them. "Men of Galilee," they said, "why do you stand here looking into the sky? This same Jesus, who has been taken from you into heaven, will come back in the same way you have seen him go into heaven (Acts 1:9-11).

Every time I read this passage I am struck by a powerful memory. I was visiting Jerusalem several years ago on a stormy day. My morning was spent in a church built over what is believed to be the site of Caiaphas' palace. Beneath the church are the remains of an ancient dungeon. Many believe that Jesus was held in this cave-like jail the night of his trial. Alongside the cell are two pillars where prisoners were chained and flogged. I can't explain how moved I felt as I pictured the Lord waiting in this place for the death sentence he knew was at hand.

I was deep in thought as I stepped out of the cathedral. Huge thunderclouds were rumbling over my head. As I looked above the walls of Jerusalem, I saw the clouds part and a bright shaft of sunlight penetrate the darkness. Immediately my heart began to pound. I thought, "This is it. It is really happening." For a handful of seconds I thought the Lord was returning. What a disappointment when the moment passed, and I realized it was only a ray of sunlight.

It's not hard to empathize with the disciples standing and watching an empty sky. It will be an awesome day when Christ returns. But until he comes,

…It is not a day for standing and watching — it is a day for seeing and waiting

Three times in Acts 1:1-11 we find the disciples focusing their sight on Jesus. In verse three, Jesus, *"after his suffering showed himself to these men."* In verse nine, *"He was taken up before their very eyes…."* And then in verse 10, *"They were looking intently up into the sky…."*

Becoming a spiritually empowered church begins with a focused vision on our living, reigning Lord. Like the disciples, we must look intently upon him. He desires to show himself to those who have eyes to see.

Put in your own words the promise Jesus Christ gave his disciples in John 14:18-20.

18"I will not leave you as orphans; I will come to you. 19Before long, the world will not see me anymore, but you will see me. Because I live, you also will live. 20On that day you will realize that I am in my Father, and you are in me, and I am in you."

— **John 14:18-20**

_____

_____

_____

This is a day for seeing Christ alive and at work! It is also a day for waiting on his Spirit. When we talk about the Great Commission, we tend to focus on the word "go." For the first disciples, however, the operative word was "wait." The Lord Jesus didn't want them to rush off and attempt ministry in their own strength.

In our case we are not waiting for the Holy Spirit to come upon the church. The baptism of the Spirit occurred in a miraculous way on Pentecost. Now every true believer receives the Spirit at the time of conversion. Yet it is still possible for us to live and serve out of our own best efforts. Churches can become merely human institutions. So we seek the empowerment of God's Spirit. We wait on him.

What did Jesus teach his disciples about seeking his Spirit? Read Luke 11:11-13. _____

_____

_____

_____

> 11"Which of you fathers, if your son asks for a fish, will give him a snake instead? 12Or if he asks for an egg, will give him a scorpion? 13If you then, though you are evil, know how to give good gifts to your children, how much more will your Father in heaven give the Holy Spirit to those who ask him!"
> — Luke 11:11-13

…It is a day for seeing and waiting — it is also a day for stepping up as his witnesses

A witness is one who gives firsthand testimony to a truth he or she has experienced. The Holy Spirit has been given so that we might know Christ and then make him known to others. Notice how Jesus explained this to his apostles in John 15:26-27. ***In your own words summarize what he taught.*** _____

_____

_____

_____

> 26"When the Counselor comes, whom I will send to you from the Father, the Spirit of truth who goes out from the Father, he will testify about me. 27And you also must testify, for you have been with me from the beginning." — John 15:26-27

What is our *Guiding Conviction?*

Christ is expanding his reign, in and through his followers, by the power of his Spirit.

John R.W. Stott, in his book *Our Guilty Silence,* tells the story of young Hudson Taylor, who was worshiping with a congregation in Brighton in 1865. Taylor was so burdened for China that he found "the self-satisfied, hymn-singing congregation intolerable." He grabbed his hat, left the worship service and went out on the beach by himself. There he prayed for 24 willing servants to join him in his efforts to reach China. John Stott makes the point that worship is "worth-ship." He writes, *"It is therefore impossible for me to worship God truly and yet not care two cents whether anybody else worships him too… Worship that is pleasing to God will inevitably send us out to bear witness of the name we have sought to honor."*

Conclude this lesson by writing down a prayer expressing how you want the Holy Spirit to work in you and your church to impact the world around you. _____

_____

_____

_____

_____

For Group Discussion

1. Jesus is expanding his reign in and through you. Describe how you are seeking the reign of Christ in your life. How are you seeing Christ's reign in the lives of others around you? (Day One)

2. Name some ways God is bringing people from other nations to our community. (Day Three)

3. How is the Lord already connecting our church with ministries in other countries? (Day Three)

4. Rate the missions temperature in our church.

+—————+—————+—————+—————+
Hot   Lukewarm   Cold
highly visible,   the special   not at all
strongly embraced   interest of few

5. Relate how the Holy Spirit is at work in your life displaying Christ's love and truth to others. (Day Four)

6. Explain how our church is bringing the living and reigning presence of Jesus into our community. (from DVD)

7. Many evangelical churches aren't quite sure how to invite the Holy Spirit's involvement into their planning, decision making, worship, selection of leaders, etc. How could we become more Spirit-empowered — reproducing disciples, leaders and congregations here and among the nations?

8. Speculate on ways our attitudes and activities might change as we increasingly recognize ourselves as part of Christ's ongoing 2000-year mission.

PRAYER POINT • As a group, pray that our church will step out and embrace Christ's mission. Pray for your own witness to those who don't know Christ.

Lesson Two

Preparing His People

Then they returned to Jerusalem from the hill called the Mount of Olives, a Sabbath day's walk from the city. 13When they arrived, they went upstairs to the room where they were staying. Those present were Peter, John, James and Andrew; Philip and Thomas, Bartholomew and Matthew; James son of Alphaeus and Simon the Zealot, and Judas son of James. 14They all joined together constantly in prayer, along with the women and Mary the mother of Jesus, and with his brothers.

Acts 1:12-14

Let me ask you one of my favorite questions: What is the largest living organism on the face of the earth? The answer may surprise you. Many believe it is an aspen grove covering hundreds of acres on the western slope of the Rocky Mountains. Aspen, for the most part, do not grow as individual trees. They grow as clusters of trees called clones. Aspen reproduce out of their root systems as shoots rise up out of the ground to form new trees. All the trees that make up a clone share the same DNA. That is why you can see whole groves of aspen changing from brilliant green to golden yellow all at the same time.

For many years I served as a pastor in Colorado. I vividly remember an experience while hiking over the Continental Divide one spring. My wife and I set up our tent in an aspen grove that evening. I woke up the following morning and stepped out of the tent just as the sun rose over the divide. The grove shimmered around me as shafts of sunlight filtered through the translucent leaves and sparkled off a million dew drops. Less

Christ expands
his reign by
preparing
his people to
reflect his glory
and reproduce
his life in others.

than 20 feet away a fawn grazed on knee-high grass intermixed with red, yellow and purple spring flowers. I felt overwhelmed by God and his creative capacity to design an ecosystem so marked by natural beauty and complex interdependence.

Now I need to tell you the truth. That huge aspen grove growing on the western slope of the Rockies is *not* the largest living organism on the face of the earth. The largest living organism is the church of Jesus Christ. Yet an aspen grove provides a vivid image of what the church is meant to be. Like aspen, we who make up Christ's church are designed by God…

- To reflect the beauty of Christ. As his Son-light shimmers through our lives, we are transformed more and more into his likeness. What if seekers stepping into your church felt as I did that spring morning when I awakened to the startling beauty of a Colorado aspen grove?

- To rise up and grow together, not as stand-alone believers, but as clusters of disciples sharing the DNA of Christ's life.

- To reproduce the life of Christ in others. Like aspen, we reproduce out of a root system deeply anchored in the soil of Christ's love and truth. Out of the shared life of the church shoots of new life spring up and reproduce in schools, neighborhoods and workplaces.

The first 15 chapters of Acts tell the story of the early church in Jerusalem. It is a remarkable case study for understanding how the Lord builds his church. In less than two decades, the "one-room" congregation we find in chapter 1 multiplied into the large global movement we see in chapter 15. The gospel witness of a small band of Galilean disciples crossed barriers of language, culture and geography. It transformed lives and communities everywhere it spread. How did that happen? The answer is found in the power of God at work in the lives of believing people. They faced external opposition, internal conflict and obstacles of every kind. Their lives and ministries were in a constant state of change as they adjusted to fresh challenges and new realities. Through it all, they persevered for the glory of God.

When Jesus ascended to heaven, he left a small circle of followers behind to establish his church. It was this gathering of believers the Holy Spirit used to reproduce disciples and multiply churches from Jerusalem to the ends of the earth. Jesus had focused more than three years of his life on preparing them to carry out his global mission.

Picture the scene Luke described in Acts 1:12-14. Imagine those 120 men and women constantly gathering to pray and prepare for the empowering work of the Holy Spirit Jesus had promised would come.

Stop and reflect on how Jesus prepared the group of disciples gathered together in the upper room. From your knowledge of the Gospel accounts, think about the various

ways Jesus invested in their lives in order to prepare them for their mission. What Jesus did to shape that first circle of disciples he is still doing to prepare his people today.

- Jesus prepares his people by calling them to follow him. It is an invitation to transforming faith.

- Jesus prepares his people by calling them to follow him together. It is an invitation to loving interdependence.

- Jesus prepares his people by calling them to go and make disciples. It is an invitation to spiritual reproduction.

Day One

Jesus prepares his people by calling them to come and follow him — it is an invitation to life-transforming faith

The same invitation Christ extended to his first disciples, he now extends to us:

- *"Come and see...."* Spending time with Christ and getting to know him personally is the "basic stuff" of discipleship. It is true for individual disciples, and it is even more true for circles of disciples who desire to grow together into a spiritually vital church. The big question for us is this, How can we make our times of worship, prayer and Bible study genuinely more about spending time with the Lord and getting to know him better?

- *"Follow me and I will make you...."* For the first disciples it meant leaving their nets in order to follow Jesus as he made them into fishers of men. It is still true for us. What will we need to leave behind to truly follow him together? What next steps of obedience will he lead us to take together? What fresh faith experiences will he lead us into that will make us the kind of church capable of casting the net and drawing in a great catch?

- *"Come and be with me...."* Life-transforming faith is not shaped in a Sunday school class. It is shaped by living life in the presence of Jesus. Christ invited his first followers to come and be with him as he shaped their faith in the midst of life. He led them into places of busy ministry and places of quiet renewal. He brought them with him as he touched the hurts of people, faced ministry critics, spread the gospel from village to village, set apart times for prayer and quiet and as he dealt with everyday tasks of life.

Daily life with Jesus was the classroom our Lord used to shape his first followers. It is the same for us. ***How can we as a circle of disciples step into our homes, our workplaces,***

our recreational settings and our circles of relationships with fresh eyes and hearts? How do we make them the real classrooms for coming and being with Jesus? _____

_____

_____

_____

_____

Think about how Jesus challenged his disciples in the midst of life's frustrations, disappointments and joys. His most frequent rebuke was "O you of little faith." His most frequent command was "Do not be afraid." He wanted them to increasingly experience him as trustworthy and to follow him joyfully with obedient faith. Spiritually vital churches are made up of people whose lives are being transformed into the beauty of Christ as they learn to follow him by faith.

The bottom-line issue is this: Are we learning to trust Jesus enough to obey his commands in our daily lives? He displays his love, courage, joy and faithfulness in our lives as we look to him in loving, obedient faith.

How are you doing? Stop and take a quick inventory.

Life Transformation — growing in faith and Christlikeness

Circle the number that best reflects your present experience, from 1 = "rarely modeling" to 5 = "consistently modeling." Use "3" as infrequently as possible.

I am secure in God's love and forgiveness through faith in Christ's cross.

1	2	3	4	5

I am growing in Christ through fresh steps of faith and obedience.

1	2	3	4	5

Christ is giving me his love for God and the people in my life.

1	2	3	4	5

I am experiencing and expressing Christ's joy in my daily circumstances.

1	2	3	4	5

I am experiencing the presence and power of the Holy Spirit in my daily life.

1	2	3	4	5

I am living in freedom and victory over secret sins.

1	2	3	4	5

I am growing in knowledge of and obedience to God's Word.

1	2	3	4	5

I am reflecting Christ's faithfulness in my commitments and responsibilities.

| 1 | 2 | 3 | 4 | 5 |

People who know me see positive changes in the past 12 months.

| 1 | 2 | 3 | 4 | 5 |

I am exercising Christ's control over my passions and desires.

| 1 | 2 | 3 | 4 | 5 |

*Reflect on the inventory and jot down specific prayer requests expressing to Christ how you want him to strengthen your faith and change your life.*_____

_____

_____

_____

_____

_____

_____

_____

Day Two

Jesus prepares his people by calling them to follow him together — it is an invitation to loving interdependence

The 120 disciples gathered in Jerusalem had all personally experienced Christ. They had also come to know Christ together as a shared experience. Jesus had given them his love and taught them how to give his love to each other. It was the desire of his heart to shape his followers into a community of disciples whose relationships reflected his love and truth.

Think about how his love for them was marked by speaking the truth in love, by demonstrating servanthood, by exercising grace and patience, by mercy and forgiveness and by laying down his life for them. Think about how he taught them when they were quibbling over who would be the greatest… about how he washed their feet…about how he rebuked the smallness of their faith while loving them into greater faith. Then

9"As the Father has loved me, so have I loved you. Now remain in my love. 10If you obey my commands, you will remain in my love, just as I have obeyed my Father's commands and remain in his love. 11I have told you this so that my joy may be in you and that your joy may be complete. 12My command is this: Love each other as I have loved you. 13Greater love has no one than this, that he lay down his life for his friends."
— **John 15:9-13**

1Brothers, if someone is caught in a sin, you who are spiritual should restore him gently. But watch yourself, or you also may be tempted. 2Carry each other's burdens, and in this way you will fulfill the law of Christ. 3If anyone thinks he is something when he is nothing, he deceives himself. 4Each one should test his own actions. Then he can take pride in himself, without comparing himself to somebody else, 5for each one should carry his own load. — **Galatians 6:1-5**

20"My prayer is not for them alone. I pray also for those who will believe in me through their message, 21that all of them may be one, Father, just as you are in me and I am in you. May they also be in us so that the world may believe that you have sent me. 22I have given them the glory that you gave me, that they may be one as we are one: 23I in them and you in me. May they be brought to complete unity to let the world know that you sent me and have loved them even as you have loved me."
— **John 17:20-23**

think about how he commanded them to "Love each other as I have loved you." Is it any different for us today as his church?

Read John 15:9-13. Put in your own words what Jesus was teaching. _____

_____

_____

_____

_____

_____

_____

_____

_____

_____

Some Christians live as if they are spiritually independent. They try to follow Christ without the support and accountability of close Christian fellowship. Others are spiritually dependent, always relying upon the strength of others. Christ taught his followers how to grow in faith through loving interdependence by helping and encouraging each other. *Study Galatians 6:1-5 and describe what is being taught about spiritual interdependence.* _____

_____

_____

_____

_____

Now, read John 17:20-23 and describe how Jesus is praying for us today. _____

_____

_____

_____

_____

_____

_____

_____

Once again take a quick personal inventory.

Loving Interdependence — growing together in Christ's love

Circle the number that best reflects your present experience, from 1 = "rarely modeling" to 5 = "consistently modeling." Use "3" as infrequently as possible.

I make priority time for building loving relationships.

    1   2   3   4   5

I share freely and honestly about my joys and struggles.

    1   2   3   4   5

I am not quick-tempered and I express anger constructively.

    1   2   3   4   5

I express my opinions without being overbearing or quarrelsome.

    1   2   3   4   5

I make every effort to keep the unity of the Spirit in the bond of peace.

    1   2   3   4   5

I honor the reputations of others by refusing to gossip or slander.

    1   2   3   4   5

I build up others by speaking the truth in love.

    1   2   3   4   5

I honor those in positions of authority and submit to their leadership.

    1   2   3   4   5

I receive instruction and correction with a teachable spirit.

    1   2   3   4   5

I value the gifts and perspectives of people from diverse backgrounds.

    1   2   3   4   5

Reflect on specific ways you want to better model Christ's love as a member of his church. Write specific prayer requests about the ways you want to grow in loving interdependence.

_____

_____

_____

_____

_____

_____

Day Three

Jesus prepares his people by calling them to go and make disciples — it is an invitation to spiritual reproduction

The community of disciples we find in Acts 1 understood that Christ was preparing them to fulfill his mission in the world. Christ's church was never meant to exist for itself. What a tragedy it would have been if they had become self-satisfied and self-serving. What if they had remained a small church of 120 people enjoying their worship and fellowship with no sense of responsibility for the surrounding community?

What if they hadn't focused their energies upward and outward to reproduce disciples and congregations across Jerusalem and around the world? Praise God that the first church took the blessing of spiritual and relational vitality and shared it with others. We must as well. Churches that lose passion and effectiveness for spiritual reproduction are in a dangerous place — a place of decline and slow death.

Congregations, like other organizations, tend to have a predictable life cycle. Churches begin life with a clear sense of mission and a high level of passion for impacting the surrounding community for Christ. Just as an infant develops into an adolescent, young churches tend to grow in numbers and ministry effectiveness. Most churches will experience a higher level of conversion growth in their first 10 years of existence than they will ever see again. As a church grows into its prime, it is marked by spiritual and relational vitality combined with strong leadership and high-impact ministries. This season of church life will be remembered in the future as the glory years.

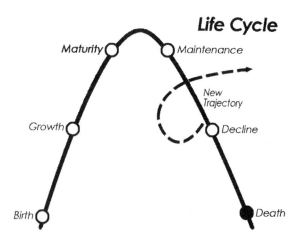

As churches mature, however, they typically major on developing facilities, improving organization, increasing ministry programs and formalizing leadership structures. In time, even the best churches tend to lose a clear sense of mission and give increasing energy to maintaining ministry programs and structures. As in all of life, when congregations stop growing, they begin to lose vitality and enter a season of decline. If a declining church fails to make life-renewing changes, death is inevitable.

What does this life-cycle reality mean for us as followers of Christ? Two responses are equally important. First, it is imperative that we make a priority of planting churches — as many as possible. Second, we need to renew existing churches for new seasons of vital, fruitful ministry. Our challenge is both to mobilize and to multiply healthy, reproducing churches.

I don't know where your church is on the congregational life cycle, but I do know you are meant to be a catalyst for spiritual reproduction. Jesus made it clear that fruitfulness is our calling.

Read John 15:1-8 with fresh eyes. How is a vital relationship with Christ connected to being fruitful, multiplying disciples? _____

_____

_____

_____

_____

Now take time again for a personal inventory.

Spiritual reproduction — growing in fruitful ministry

Circle the number that best reflects your present experience, from 1 = "rarely modeling" to 5 = "consistently modeling." Use "3" as infrequently as possible.

I am building friendships with unbelievers and sharing Christ's love and truth.
| 1 | 2 | 3 | 4 | 5 |

I am making a priority of helping my family members love and follow Christ.
| 1 | 2 | 3 | 4 | 5 |

I know my spiritual gifts and am using them to build up the body of Christ.
| 1 | 2 | 3 | 4 | 5 |

I have a clear sense of God's calling and purpose for my life.
| 1 | 2 | 3 | 4 | 5 |

I believe in the power of prayer to change lives and regularly intercede for others.
| 1 | 2 | 3 | 4 | 5 |

I love to join my gifts and efforts with others to work together as a team.
| 1 | 2 | 3 | 4 | 5 |

I demonstrate a servant spirit, assisting others without a need for recognition.
| 1 | 2 | 3 | 4 | 5 |

I am grounded in Scripture and sound doctrine, so I might instruct and correct.
| 1 | 2 | 3 | 4 | 5 |

1"I am the true vine, and my Father is the gardener. 2He cuts off every branch In me that bears no fruit, while every branch that does bear fruit he prunes so that it will be even more fruitful. 3You are already clean because of the word I have spoken to you. 4Remain in me, and I will remain in you. No branch can bear fruit by itself; it must remain in the vine. Neither can you bear fruit unless you remain in me.

5"I am the vine; you are the branches. If a man remains in me and I in him, he will bear much fruit; apart from me you can do nothing. 6If anyone does not remain in me, he is like a branch that is thrown away and withers; such branches are picked up, thrown into the fire and burned. 7If you remain in me and my words remain in you, ask whatever you wish, and it will be given you. 8This is to my Father's glory, that you bear much fruit, showing yourselves to be my disciples." — **John 15:1-8**

15In those days Peter stood up among the believers (a group numbering about a hundred and twenty) 16and said, "Brothers, the Scripture had to be fulfilled which the Holy Spirit spoke long ago through the mouth of David concerning Judas, who served as guide for those who arrested Jesus— 17he was one of our number and shared in this ministry."

18(With the reward he got for his wickedness, Judas bought a field; there he fell headlong, his body burst open and all his intestines spilled out. 19Everyone in Jerusalem heard about this, so they called that field in their language Akeldama, that is, Field of Blood.)

20"For," said Peter, "it is written in the book of Psalms,
" 'May his place be deserted;
let there be no one to
dwell in it,' and,
" 'May another take his
place of leadership.'
21"Therefore it is necessary to choose one of the men who have been with us the whole time the Lord Jesus went in and out among us, 22beginning from John's baptism to the time when Jesus was taken up from us. For one of these must become a witness with us of his resurrection."

23So they proposed two men: Joseph called Barsabbas (also known as Justus) and Matthias. 24Then they prayed, "Lord, you know everyone's heart. Show us which of these two you have chosen 25to take over this apostolic ministry, which Judas left to go where he belongs." 26Then they cast lots, and the lot fell to Matthias; so he was added to the eleven apostles.

— Acts 1:15-26

I identify emerging leaders and invest in their growth and development.

| 1 | 2 | 3 | 4 | 5 |

I love to enfold new people into relationships where they can grow in Christ.

| 1 | 2 | 3 | 4 | 5 |

What steps does Christ want you to take toward greater fruitfulness? Write specific prayer requests. _____

_____

_____

_____

_____

Day Four

Becoming a vital, reproducing church requires vital, reproducing leaders

One of the first tasks of the early church in Jerusalem was to choose a spiritual leader to replace Judas and serve alongside the remaining 11 apostles. It is impossible to overstate the importance of the apostles' role in leading the church to faithfulness and fruitfulness. They modeled, taught and nurtured spiritual and relational vitality. They led the church toward the kind of risk-taking faith that resulted in disciples and congregations being multiplied around the world. Selecting and following the right spiritual leaders was essential then, and it is essential now.

Read Acts 1:15-26 and reflect on what happened:

How was God's Word used? _____

_____

_____

What qualifications did they look for? _____

_____

_____

What part did prayer play? _____

_____

_____

What do you think of the method they used to choose between Justus and Matthias? Why do you think they did it that way? _____

_____

_____

_____

_____

For the early church, selecting the right apostle was part human discernment and part divine guidance. We don't select apostles today, but we still need both discernment and guidance to raise the leaders who oversee and shepherd our churches.

Over the past few days we focused on how Jesus prepares his disciples in the three areas of transforming faith, loving interdependence and spiritual reproduction. *What kind of leadership do you think a congregation needs in order to grow in…*

Life-transforming faith? _____

_____

_____

_____

Loving interdependence? _____

_____

_____

_____

Spiritual reproduction? _____

_____

_____

_____

Close by jotting down how you want to pray for the spiritual leaders in your church.

_____

_____

_____

_____

_____

_____

_____

Day Five

Channeling desires into disciplines

We can't leave the subject of preparing Christ's people without determining a pathway for growth. Inherent in the word *disciple* is the word *discipline*. I am sure each of us desires to grow in life-transforming faith, loving interdependence and spiritual reproduction. Now we need to channel our desires into disciplines. Take a moment for one last inventory:

Spiritual Disciplines — the means for growing spiritual and relational vitality

Circle the number that best reflects your present experience, from 1 = "rarely modeling" to 5 = "consistently modeling." Use "3" as infrequently as possible.

I am experiencing spiritual growth by participating in a vital small group.

1	2	3	4	5

Worshiping the Lord is a central and joyful part of my life.

1	2	3	4	5

I spend quality, regular time reading and reflecting on God's Word.

1	2	3	4	5

I am enjoying a meaningful prayer life, praising and trusting the Lord.

1	2	3	4	5

I am honoring Christ as a good steward of my time, money and abilities.

1	2	3	4	5

Review your spiritual inventories from the past five days and identify your key growth areas.

I am praying for growth in the following areas:

Transforming Faith	Loving Interdependence	Spiritual Reproduction

What spiritual disciplines will help me grow in Christ? _____

_____

_____

The early church was committed to the spiritual discipline of praying together. Luke wrote, *"They all joined together constantly in prayer"* (Acts 1:14). One of the most powerful things you could do is to find a prayer partner or two and pray regularly for each other and for your church. Praying together brings accountability, encouragement and shared faith to the process of growing in Christ.

Christ expands
his reign by
preparing
his people to
reflect his glory
and reproduce
his life in others.

Who should I ask to be my prayer partners? _____

_____

_____

_____

When can we find time to pray together in person or on the phone? _____

_____

_____

_____

Now the adventure really begins. I can almost visualize you springing up like a shoot of new life — rooted in Christ — rising up alongside a cluster of growing disciples, reflecting Christ's beauty and reproducing his life in others.

For Group Discussion

1. How can our church make our times of prayer, Bible study and worship genuinely more about spending time with the Lord — getting to know him better? (Day One)

2. Name some ways we can make our workplaces into real classrooms for being with Jesus. Our recreational settings. Our circles of relationships. (Day One)

3. On the DVD segment, Jerry Sheveland said, "We really can't embrace Christ's mission until we embrace Christ's church." Discuss whether you agree or disagree.

4. Christ calls us to loving interdependence. How loving is our church? How well have we learned to depend on one another? Give an example.

5. In your opinion, how committed are we as a church to reproducing new disciples?

   +———————-+—————————+—————————+
   Promising   Improving   Struggling   Indifferent

6. Tell any insights you gained by looking at the "Life Cycle" of a church. (Day Three) Where is our church in its life cycle?

7. Evaluate: How effective is our church in reproducing vital disciples? Leaders? New churches? (Day Four)

8. Describe your progress in finding one or more prayer partners and establishing a schedule to pray together.

PRAYER POINT • Pray for the church's passion and effectiveness in making new disciples. Pray that all in the group grow in their daily walk with Jesus.

Lesson Three

Empowered by His Spirit

When the day of Pentecost came, they were all together in one place. ²Suddenly a sound like the blowing of a violent wind came from heaven and filled the whole house where they were sitting. ³They saw what seemed to be tongues of fire that separated and came to rest on each of them. ⁴All of them were filled with the Holy Spirit and began to speak in other tongues as the Spirit enabled them.

⁵Now there were staying in Jerusalem God-fearing Jews from every nation under heaven. ⁶When they heard this sound, a crowd came together in bewilderment, because each one heard them speaking in his own language. ⁷Utterly amazed, they asked: "Are not all these men who are speaking Galileans? ⁸Then how is it that each of us hears them in his own native language? ⁹Parthians, Medes and Elamites; residents of Mesopotamia, Judea and Cappadocia, Pontus and Asia, ¹⁰Phrygia and Pamphylia, Egypt and the parts of Libya near Cyrene; visitors from Rome ¹¹(both Jews and converts to Judaism); Cretans and Arabs — we hear them declaring the wonders of God in our own tongues!" ¹²Amazed and perplexed, they asked one another, "What does this mean?"

Acts 2:1-12

In today's church we celebrate the "Big Six" in a big way: Christmas, Palm Sunday, Good Friday, Easter, Mother's Day and Thanksgiving. We would throw in Independence Day, but attendance is pretty slim around the Fourth of July. What we surprisingly neglect is our own birthday — the day the New Testament church was born. The day, of course, is called "Pentecost." This neglect would be inconsequential if it were not for the fact that Pentecost is God's powerful reminder of why the church exists in the world. Everything about Pentecost tells us our primary reason for being is to glorify God

among the nations in the power of his Spirit. To underscore the point, God provided three signs:

1. **The Sign of the Wind: Filling Us with His Life** — *Suddenly a sound like the blowing of a violent wind came from heaven and filled the whole house where they were sitting* (Acts 2:2).

2. **The Sign of Fire: Indwelling Us with His Presence** — *They saw what seemed to be tongues of fire that separated and came to rest on each of them* (Acts 2:3).

3. **The Sign of the Languages: Empowering Us for Witness** — *All of them were filled with the Holy Spirit and began to speak in other tongues as the Spirit enabled them* (Acts 2:4).

Key truths about the Holy Spirit

What do we need to know about the Holy Spirit in order to understand his presence and power in our lives? Jesus prepared his disciples by teaching them about the Spirit who would come. The Gospel of John records several key truths about the Holy Spirit that Jesus taught in the days leading up to his crucifixion.

1. **The Holy Spirit is sent to be our counselor** — literally, one called to stand by our side — just as Jesus was with his first disciples. *And I will ask the Father, and he will give you another Counselor to be with you forever...* (John 14:16).

2. **The Holy Spirit is the personal presence of Christ living with us and in us.** *But you know him, for he lives with you and will be in you. I will not leave you as orphans; I will come to you* (John 14:17-18).

3. **The Holy Spirit is the Spirit of truth** who teaches and guides us in the truth of Christ. *When the Counselor comes, whom I will send to you from the Father, the Spirit of truth who goes out from the Father, he will testify about me* (John 15:26).

4. **The Holy Spirit is also sent to convict the world of its need of Christ.** *When he comes, he will convict the world of guilt in regard to sin and righteousness and judgment...* (John 16:8).

5. **The Holy Spirit comes to help Christ's followers be his witnesses.** *...he will testify about me. And you also must testify, for you have been with me from the beginning* (John 15:26-27).

6. **The Holy Spirit has come to bring glory to Christ.** *He will bring glory to me by taking from what is mine and making it known to you* (John 16:14).

What are we meant to understand about the Holy Spirit? He is the Spirit of God — one with God the Father and God the Son. He has been sent to glorify Christ by empowering his followers and convicting the world. He brings the personal presence of Christ into our lives. He is our indwelling counselor, teacher and guide. He helps us know and experience all that is ours in Jesus Christ.

> Christ empowers his people to expand his reign through the personal presence of his Spirit.

Do you feel the breath of a mighty wind blowing across your soul? Do you sense the inner glow of a glorious presence? Is there a word rising on your tongue ready to bound over linguistic, geographical and cultural barriers to reach the ears of one who needs to hear? In the light of the Pentecost mandate, all of us as followers of Christ are given his Spirit to empower our shared mission as his church.

Day One

The sign of the wind: filling us with his life

Suddenly a sound like the blowing of a violent wind came from heaven and filled the whole house where they were sitting (Acts 2:2).

To understand the sign of the wind one must know that the word for *wind* is the same word used for both *breath* and *soul*. When God created Adam, we are told that he *"…formed the man from the dust of the ground and breathed into his nostrils the breath of life, and the man became a living being"* (Gen. 2:7). Man was merely a physical entity until God blew the breath of life into his lungs. It was then that he became a living being. So it was with Christ's church. The Holy Spirit filled the place where the believers were assembled with the sound of a mighty wind — together they became the body of Christ, alive with his Spirit.

Jesus used the image of wind to explain what it means to be born again.
The wind blows wherever it pleases. You hear its sound, but you cannot tell where it comes from or where it is going. So it is with everyone born of the Spirit (John 3:8).

Like the wind that is invisible to the eye yet blows where it wills, so Christ's Spirit breathes new life into those once dead to God but now alive in Christ. We see this truth emphasized at Pentecost with the sign of rushing wind.

Receiving the life of his Spirit

It is time to make this matter of Christ's empowering Spirit a personal one. *What promise did Peter make to us in Acts 2:38-39 about receiving the Holy Spirit?*

_____

_____

When does the Holy Spirit enter our lives to indwell and empower us? (Ephesians 1:13-14.)

_____

_____

38Peter replied, "Repent and be baptized, every one of you, in the name of Jesus Christ for the forgiveness of your sins. And you will receive the gift of the Holy Spirit. 39The promise is for you and your children and for all who are far off—for all whom the Lord our God will call."
— **Acts 2:38-39**

13And you also were included in Christ when you heard the word of truth, the gospel of your salvation. Having believed, you were marked in him with a seal, the promised Holy Spirit, 14who is a deposit guaranteeing our inheritance until the redemption of those who are God's possession—to the praise of his glory.
—**Ephesians 1:13-14**

Do not get drunk on wine, which leads to debauchery. Instead, be filled with the Spirit. —Ephesians 5:18

9"So I say to you: Ask and it will be given to you; seek and you will find; knock and the door will be opened to you. 10For everyone who asks receives; he who seeks finds; and to him who knocks, the door will be opened.

11"Which of you fathers, if your son asks for a fish, will give him a snake instead? 12Or if he asks for an egg, will give him a scorpion? 13If you then, though you are evil, know how to give good gifts to your children, how much more will your Father in heaven give the Holy Spirit to those who ask him!"

— Luke 11:9-13

The Holy Spirit can be present in us but not filling us with his power. What did Paul teach in Ephesians 5:18? _____

_____

_____

What did Jesus promise in Luke 11:9-13 about seeking the presence and power of the Holy Spirit? _____

_____

_____

_____

The Old Testament prophet Ezekiel was given a powerful vision of God breathing new life into his people. In this vision the house of Israel appeared as a valley filled with dry bones. God asked Ezekiel, "…*can these bones live?*" The prophet responded, "*O Sovereign Lord, you alone know.*" As the vision unfolded, the Lord caused the dry bones to reconnect and then be covered with tendons, flesh and skin — but there was no breath in them. The Lord instructed Ezekiel to prophesy to the four winds to breathe life into the slain. This is how Ezekiel reported what he saw in the vision:

So I prophesied as he commanded me, and breath entered them; they came to life and stood up on their feet — a vast army (Ezek. 37:10).

This particular prophecy was about the Lord's promise to restore the nation of Israel. Yet in a powerful way it pictures what happened at Pentecost. The Lord breathed his life into his church and it stood up — the living body of Christ.

It may be that the Lord is asking you the same question he asked Ezekiel, "Can these bones live?" Can I breathe fresh life into your soul… your church… your community… your world?

Close today's study by asking the Father for the fullness of his Spirit just as if you were a hungry child asking your mom or dad for a peanut butter-and-jelly sandwich. *Put your prayer into words.* _____

_____

_____

_____

_____

Day Two

The sign of fire:
indwelling us with his presence

They saw what seemed to be tongues of fire that separated and came to rest on each of them (Acts 2:3).

You cannot know the story of Israel's history without also knowing about the "Shekinah glory." The word *Shekinah* literally means "that which dwells," and it refers to the abiding presence of the Lord in all his glory. This "Shekinah glory" or "God's glorious presence" was often displayed to Israel by fire and light.

- The fire in Moses' bush

- The pillar of fire leading Israel in the wilderness

- The Shekinah glow that remained on Moses' face long after he was with God on the mountain

- The fire that came down from heaven and filled Solomon's temple with glory when it was completed

The New Testament has its own examples:

- The glory of God glowed around the angels announcing the coming of Christ and a star shone over Bethlehem.

- Jesus was transfigured on the mountain and glowed with the light of glory.

- A common word picture for Christ coming into the world is "light in the darkness."

- The Book of Revelation says we will need no sun in heaven because the light from Jesus' shining glory will be enough.

On Pentecost the Shekinah glory fell as tongues of fire on every believer. The sign is brilliantly clear. The glorious presence of God abides in each believer as that believer goes out into a dark world.

No longer does the Shekinah glory dwell in a temple building or shine in a tabernacle tent. In the season of the New Testament church, God doesn't say come to the building or the tent where my glory dwells. He proclaims to those who bear the Shekinah to go and bring it to the nations.

Jesus has given us the Holy Spirit so that he might display his glorious presence in our lives. He wants to shine through us to the world around us. ***What did he teach in Matthew 5:14-16?*** _____

_____

_____

14"You are the light of the world. A city on a hill cannot be hidden. 15Neither do people light a lamp and put it under a bowl. Instead they put it on its stand, and it gives light to everyone in the house. 16In the same way, let your light shine before men, that they may see your good deeds and praise your Father in heaven."

—Matthew 5:14-16

9But you are a chosen people, a royal priesthood, a holy nation, a people belonging to God, that you may declare the praises of him who called you out of darkness into his wonderful light. 10Once you were not a people, but now you are the people of God; once you had not received mercy, but now you have received mercy.

11Dear friends, I urge you, as aliens and strangers in the world, to abstain from sinful desires, which war against your soul. 12Live such good lives among the pagans that, though they accuse you of doing wrong, they may see your good deeds and glorify God on the day he visits us.

—1 Peter 2:9-12

The Spirit of Christ fell on the whole church. He empowers the church to display the glory of the Lord in its worship, fellowship and witness. *What did Peter teach about us as a people "called out of darkness into his wonderful light"? (See 1 Peter 2:9-12.)*

_____

_____

_____

_____

Everything about a Spirit-filled church declares before a watching community: "Jesus is alive and reigning in our midst." The Holy Spirit makes the life of Christ real in us and gives us the power to see Christ's life reproduced in others. It is Christ's passion to see spiritually vital churches mobilized and multiplied throughout the world so that God's glory might be displayed among the nations.

No wonder in Matthew 28 Jesus precedes the Great Commission by saying, *"All authority on heaven and earth has been given unto me...."* And no wonder he concludes the Commission with the promise, *"And surely I am with you always, to the very end of the age."*

How do you want Jesus to shine his glory through your church in a greater way in the power of his Spirit? _____

_____

_____

_____

_____

Day Three

The sign of the languages: empowering us for witness

All of them were filled with the Holy Spirit and began to speak in other tongues as the Spirit enabled them (Acts 2:4).

With all the debate that has surrounded the issue of "tongues-speaking," we have largely missed the primary purpose of the sign. The Jews who gathered in Jerusalem didn't need the gospel preached in other languages to understand the message. Peter preached in Aramaic, and the multitude was capable of intelligent response. And the believers didn't need another language (even a heavenly language) to adequately praise God. There was a twofold message in this miracle of languages.

First, Peter in Acts 2:14-18 pointed to the fact that every believer was praising and prophesying with a special anointing. Not just men, but women too. Not just elders, but also the young. Peter pointed out it was a sign that God's Spirit had just been poured out on all people. The universal anointing of the Spirit in a supernatural way indicated the witness of the church was for all believers, not some.

Second, Peter rightly concluded it meant *"everyone who calls on the name of the Lord will be saved"* (Acts 2:21). The context shows he meant languages, cultures, ethnicity, geography, gender and age are not barriers to the gospel. The rest of the Book of Acts demonstrates how hard it was for the Jewish believers to accept that fact and get on with the mission of multiplying disciples and churches among all nations and tribes.

It is significant that the Lord chose Pentecost as the day to send his Spirit to empower the witness of his people. The Pentecost celebration was the second of Israel's three great pilgrimage feasts. It concluded a cycle of time begun at Passover, and it was named *Pentecost* because it fell on the 50th day after the offering of the barley sheaf during the Passover celebration.

The feast was designated the "day of first fruits" because it marked the beginning of the time in which God's people were to bring their offerings of first fruits to the Lord.

The meaning of the "first fruits celebration" is evident in Acts 2:40-41, where 3000 people gathered from the nations respond in faith to Peter's Pentecost sermon. They were the first fruits of the harvest that would come.

Pentecost tells us the season of the New Testament church began with the first fruits of the 3000, and it will conclude when the harvest is complete — when all nations receive the gospel.

14Then Peter stood up with the Eleven, raised his voice and addressed the crowd: "Fellow Jews and all of you who live in Jerusalem, let me explain this to you; listen carefully to what I say. 15These men are not drunk, as you suppose. It's only nine in the morning! 16No, this is what was spoken by the prophet Joel:

17"'In the last days, God says,
    I will pour out my Spirit
        on all people.
    Your sons and daughters
        will prophesy,
    your young men will
        see visions,
    your old men will
        dream dreams.
18Even on my servants, both
    men and women,
    I will pour out my Spirit
        in those days,
    and they will prophesy.
19I will show wonders in the
    heaven above
    and signs on the earth
        below,
    blood and fire and billows
        of smoke.
20The sun will be turned to
    darkness
    and the moon to blood
    before the coming of the
        great and glorious day
        of the Lord.
21And everyone who calls
    on the name of the Lord
    will be saved.'"
            —Acts 2:14-21

What does this mean?

We are told that those who heard the disciples praising God in their own languages were amazed and perplexed. They asked the right question: "What does this mean?" Peter explained by quoting the prophet Joel. *Read Acts 2:14-21 and describe in your own words what Peter wanted the Pentecost listeners to understand.* _____

_____

_____

_____

_____

Pentecost marked the first day of what Joel called the "last days." The pouring out of the Holy Spirit on all believers opened a new chapter of God's plan that would culminate in the great and glorious day of the Lord. We live in the last days. The clock is ticking. His coming is at hand. *Why do you think you and I should be urgent about being Spirit-filled followers of Christ? And why do you think your church should be urgent about growing in spiritual power?* _____

_____

_____

_____

_____

How do you think the Holy Spirit wants to work in your life to make your faith more contagious to others? _____

_____

_____

_____

How do you think the Spirit wants to work in your church to get the gospel message out in powerful ways? _____

_____

_____

_____

_____

Day Four

Proclaiming Jesus — both Lord and Christ

When Peter quoted Joel, he ended with these words:

And everyone who calls on the name of the Lord will be saved (Acts 2:21).

As he spoke these words, Peter looked into the faces of Jewish worshipers gathered in Jerusalem from all over the world. He knew there was a message from God they needed to hear. It was a message of salvation for all who call on the name of the Lord. Peter launched his message by saying, "Men of Israel, listen to this...."

22"Men of Israel, listen to this: Jesus of Nazareth was a man accredited by God to you by miracles, wonders and signs, which God did among you through him, as you yourselves know. 23This man was handed over to you by God's set purpose and foreknowledge; and you, with the help of wicked men, put him to death by nailing him to the cross. 24But God raised him from the dead, freeing him from the agony of death, because it was impossible for death to keep its hold on him. 25David said about him:

"'I saw the Lord always before me.
Because he is at my right hand,
I will not be shaken.
26Therefore my heart is glad and my tongue rejoices;
my body also will live in hope,
27because you will not abandon me to the grave,
nor will you let your Holy One see decay.
28You have made known to me the paths of life;
you will fill me with joy in your presence.'

29"Brothers, I can tell you confidently that the patriarch David died and was buried, and his tomb is here to this day. 30But he was a prophet and knew that God had promised him on oath that he would place one of his descendants on his throne. 31Seeing what was ahead, he spoke of the resurrection of the Christ, that he was not abandoned to the grave, nor did his body see decay. 32God has raised this Jesus to life, and we are all witnesses of the fact. 33Exalted to the right hand of God, he has received from the Father the promised Holy Spirit and has poured out what you now see and hear. 34For David did not ascend to heaven, and yet he said,

"'The Lord said to my Lord:
"Sit at my right hand
35until I make your enemies
a footstool for your feet." '
36"Therefore let all Israel be assured of this: God has made this Jesus, whom you crucified, both Lord and Christ."   **—Acts 2:22-36**

Read Acts 2:22-36. List the key points Peter wanted his listeners to understand and believe about Jesus: _____

_____

_____

_____

_____

_____

_____

What shall we do?

The gospel message requires a response. No one can remain neutral when confronted with the truth that Jesus is both Lord and Christ. The Holy Spirit not only empowers the gospel message — he empowers people to respond in repentance and faith. It happened at Pentecost in a graphic way.

> *When the people heard this, they were cut to the heart and said to Peter and the other apostles, "Brothers, what shall we do?"* (Acts 2:37).

At this very moment, there are people in your circle of influence who are being prepared by the Lord to ask that same question about Jesus: What shall we do? God's Spirit is at work in you and in them to bring about a faith response to Christ.

Read Acts 2:37-41 and summarize how Peter answered their question. _____
_____
_____
_____
_____

37When the people heard this, they were cut to the heart and said to Peter and the other apostles, "Brothers, what shall we do?"

38Peter replied, "Repent and be baptized, every one of you, in the name of Jesus Christ for the forgiveness of your sins. And you will receive the gift of the Holy Spirit. 39The promise is for you and your children and for all who are far off—for all whom the Lord our God will call."

40With many other words he warned them; and he pleaded with them, "Save yourselves from this corrupt generation." 41Those who accepted his message were baptized, and about three thousand were added to their number that day.

—**Acts 2:37-41**

Peter went beyond answering their "what shall we do?" question. He warned them and pleaded with them, *"Save yourself from this corrupt generation."* Three thousand responded in faith and were baptized and added to the church. What a miraculous response! It takes a miracle for anyone to be saved from this corrupt generation through faith in Christ. It takes a work of God's Spirit. It also takes witnesses who trust God's Spirit to do his work in the lives of people.

Let's be honest. It is our lack of faith in the power of God's Spirit that holds us back. As individual believers we let feelings of inadequacy and fears of rejection silence our witness. As churches we grow inward and self-centered because we really don't believe the Holy Spirit can use us to impact the surrounding community.

Take a few moments for repentance. How do you need Christ's forgiveness for doubting the power of his Spirit? _____
_____
_____
_____
_____
_____
_____

Day Five

Living in the Spirit

Bill Bright, the founder of Campus Crusade for Christ, loved to talk about spiritual breathing — exhaling self and inhaling the Spirit. It is the day-by-day, moment-by-moment process of putting off a self-on-the-throne mind-set and putting on a heart of trust in the reigning presence of Christ. Here is how the apostle Paul described it:

14The entire law is summed up in a single command: "Love your neighbor as yourself." 15If you keep on biting and devouring each other, watch out or you will be destroyed by each other.

16So I say, live by the Spirit, and you will not gratify the desires of the sinful nature. 17For the sinful nature desires what is contrary to the Spirit, and the Spirit what is contrary to the sinful nature. They are in conflict with each other, so that you do not do what you want. 18But if you are led by the Spirit, you are not under law.

19The acts of the sinful nature are obvious: sexual immorality, impurity and debauchery; 20idolatry and witchcraft; hatred, discord, jealousy, fits of rage, selfish ambition, dissensions, factions 21and envy; drunkenness, orgies, and the like. I warn you, as I did before, that those who live like this will not inherit the kingdom of God.

22But the fruit of the Spirit is love, joy, peace, patience, kindness, goodness, faithfulness, 23gentleness and self-control. Against such things there is no law. 24Those who belong to Christ Jesus have crucified the sinful nature with its passions and desires. 25Since we live by the Spirit, let us keep in step with the Spirit. 26Let us not become conceited, provoking and envying each other.

—**Galatians 5:14-26**

How did Paul explain this daily process of living in the Spirit? (Galatians 5:14-26.)

_____

_____

_____

_____

_____

The other day I found myself trapped in an airport with a cancelled flight. People all around me were expressing anger, frustration and impatience. I felt all the same impulses as I struggled with anxiety over appointments that now seemed impossible to keep. The Holy Spirit reminded me of Philippians 4:5:

Do not be anxious about anything, but in everything, by prayer and petition, with thanksgiving, present your requests to God.

In obedience, I breathed out my spirit of anxiety by asking the Lord to forgive me and by releasing my desire to be in control. I breathed in the peace of his Spirit by thankfully giving the situation over to the Lord. As I reflected on the experience, I wondered how often my witness has been damaged by acting out of anxiety instead of the peace of Christ's Spirit.

²⁹Do not let any unwholesome talk come out of your mouths, but only what is helpful for building others up according to their needs, that it may benefit those who listen. ³⁰And do not grieve the Holy Spirit of God, with whom you were sealed for the day of redemption. ³¹Get rid of all bitterness, rage and anger, brawling and slander, along with every form of malice. ³²Be kind and compassionate to one another, forgiving each other, just as in Christ God forgave you.

    —Ephesians 4:29-32

¹⁶Be joyful always; ¹⁷pray continually; ¹⁸give thanks in all circumstances, for this is God's will for you in Christ Jesus.

  ¹⁹Do not put out the Spirit's fire; ²⁰do not treat prophecies with contempt. ²¹Test everything. Hold on to the good. ²²Avoid every kind of evil.

  ²³May God himself, the God of peace, sanctify you through and through. May your whole spirit, soul and body be kept blameless at the coming of our Lord Jesus Christ. ²⁴The one who calls you is faithful and he will do it. **—1 Thessalonians 5:16-24**

Paul described two examples of how we either grieve or quench the Holy Spirit. *What do these two examples say to you about hindering the Holy Spirit's work in your life?*
Ephesians 4:29-32 _____

_____

_____

1 Thessalonians 5:16-24 _____

_____

_____

Why not do some spiritual breathing right now? What do you need to breathe out? What do you need to breathe in? _____

_____

_____

_____

_____

_____

Can you image how refreshing it would be for people in your community to witness a church filled with believers who experience and express the power of Christ's Spirit? Join me in praying, "Lord, let it begin with us. Breathe your life into us. Let the glory of your presence shine. Loosen our tongues to speak boldly, lovingly and honestly. Fill us with your Spirit."

What is our
Guiding Conviction?

Christ empowers
his people to
expand his reign
through the
personal
presence
of his Spirit.

For Group Discussion

1. When God sent his Spirit, he gave three signs that remind us why we're the church. Summarize what it means to be filled with life by the Spirit, indwelt by his presence and empowered for witness.

2. Explain: Why should you and I be urgent about being Spirit-filled followers of Christ? (Day Two)

3. In the Book of Acts, the Holy Spirit leaps over every barrier he encounters: language, culture, enthnicity, geography, gender, age. (Day Three) What's a recent example of this in our church?

4. Evaluate: What do visitors to our church say they find most attractive? In what ways might they sense Jesus alive and reigning among us?

5. Who do you know in your circle of influence that the Lord might be preparing to hear that Jesus is both Lord and Christ? (Day Four)

6. Discuss why many believers feel inadequate and fearful about allowing the Holy Spirit to witness through them. How do churches become self-centered and timid about reaching their community?

7. Because Jesus is present in us through the Holy Spirit, we are the living, breathing body of Jesus in the world. Discuss: Are we a Spirit-empowered church? How can we tell?

PRAYER POINT • Let's stop now and ask God's forgiveness for hindering his Spirit's work in us. Let's ask him to breathe his life into us for his work.

Lesson Four
Becoming His Church

They devoted themselves to the apostles' teaching and to the fellowship, to the breaking of bread and to prayer. ⁴³Everyone was filled with awe, and many wonders and miraculous signs were done by the apostles. ⁴⁴All the believers were together and had everything in common. ⁴⁵Selling their possessions and goods, they gave to anyone as he had need. ⁴⁶Every day they continued to meet together in the temple courts. They broke bread in their homes and ate together with glad and sincere hearts, ⁴⁷praising God and enjoying the favor of all the people. And the Lord added to their number daily those who were being saved.

Acts 2:42-47

Beyond passion to devotion

The operative word for the first chapter of Acts is the word *wait*. Christ entrusted his church with a clear mandate: "…*you will be my witnesses in Jerusalem, and in all Judea and Samaria, and to the ends of the earth.*" His marching orders, however, were accompanied by a command to "wait" for the gift of the Holy Spirit. Jesus didn't want his followers to rush out and attempt to accomplish their mission through human energy and effort. When the day of Pentecost arrived, the Holy Spirit filled the Jerusalem church. The presence and power of the Spirit produced a community of believers marked by spiritual and relational vitality. The contagious quality of their faith and love turned Jerusalem upside down and ultimately changed the world.

Christ is expanding his reign by raising up and reproducing Spirit-filled churches.

If you ever wondered what a Spirit-filled church really looks like, all you have to do is read the description of the Jerusalem church in Acts 2:42-47. This was not, of course, a perfect church. It was made up of hundreds of new believers with a great deal to learn. But their faith was real and their love and joy were contagious.

When we use a term like "Spirit-filled," we tend to picture passionate spirituality and emotionally expressive worship. The word that best describes the Jerusalem church, however, is not "passion" but "devotion." That's the word Luke used when he wrote…
> *They devoted themselves to the apostles' teaching and to the fellowship, to the breaking of bread and to prayer* (Acts 2:42).

Passion matters. It describes what captivates our hearts… our desires… our affections. Yet passion without devotion is only empty zeal. I have many passions in my life. Playing golf is one of them. If you were to play a round of golf with me, you would quickly discover that for me golf is a passion but not a devotion.

I don't take lessons. I don't get to the driving range. I don't play regularly. And it shows. Golf is a passion, not a devotion, in my life.

In the early church we see the Holy Spirit produced a faith that was both devoted and passionate. The apostle James, brother of Jesus, became one of the key leaders of the Jerusalem church. He later wrote a letter warning against false faith that disconnects belief from behavior. In *The Message,* Eugene Peterson paraphrased James' warning:
> *Don't fool yourself into thinking that you are a listener when you are anything but, letting the Word go in one ear and out the other. Act on what you hear!… Anyone who sets himself up as "religious" by talking a good game is self-deceived.… Real religion, the kind that passes muster before God the Father, is this: Reach out to the homeless and loveless in their plight, and guard against corruption from the godless world* (James 1:22-27).

It is important for churches to sort out what is going to matter most to them as congregations. It is a good thing for a church to write a statement of mission, vision and values. Unfortunately, what we aspire to value on a piece of paper may not be visible in our daily practices — our devotions. How we integrate our beliefs, our values and our behavior will shape our true devotion.

Recently I spoke at New Covenant Church in Knoxville, Iowa. Five years ago the Knoxville Church had declined to 17 worshipers and was considering closing its doors. At that time Craig Bex and his wife Olga began a part-time ministry pastoring the church on weekends — until it would close. They traveled 100 miles every weekend to serve the struggling congregation. Together, the remaining members of New Covenant began to wrestle with a critical question: What kind of church is needed to impact a community like Knoxville for Christ's kingdom? They understood that Knoxville was a blue-collar community marked by real needs. And they knew that Bible-teaching churches in Knoxville were too often perceived to be legalistic and condemning in nature.

Passion matters. It describes what captivates our hearts… our desires … our affections. Yet passion without devotion is only empty zeal.

A seed of conviction began to grow in their hearts. They felt called to minister to the needs of people in Knoxville with a spirit of loving grace. More important, they became devoted to that conviction and began to live it out through practical ministries. Soon a spirit of grace and loving ministry began to pervade their worship, fellowship and reputation in the community. The Sunday morning I preached at New Covenant I witnessed a congregation that had grown from 17 to 200 in five years. I also witnessed a church family living out its devotion in practical, visible ways.

The Knoxville story illustrates an important truth about our beliefs and values: If you can't see it, it's not real. Our devotions are visible for all to see. Let me ask you a couple of questions:

- If the people in your life were to look closely at your use of time, energy and finances, what would they say are your greatest devotions?

- If visitors and new attendees were to describe your church with fresh eyes, what would they say are the real devotions of your congregation?

We know what people saw when they experienced the life of the Jerusalem church. Luke described their four devotions in this way:

> They devoted themselves to the apostles' teaching and to the fellowship, to the breaking of bread and to prayer (Acts 2:42).

I like to use an acronym to describe the four devotions of the ACTS church:

Apostolic Teaching. We know from the New Testament writings that the apostles' teaching was marked by both God-centered doctrine and life application. Spirit-filled churches trust the accumulative effect of biblical preaching and teaching that connects the hearts of people to the great truths of God. Their devotion goes beyond hearing the Word to putting it into daily practice.

Caring Fellowship. The early church was not just devoted to fellowship; they were devoted to *the* fellowship. They were devoted to each other and to the common good of the church. Their devotion was lived out through practical acts of kindness and generosity. Passages like Romans 12:9-13, 1 Corinthians 13, Ephesians 4:29-32 and Colossians 3:12-17 characterize what relational vitality looks like for the church.

Transforming Worship. The Lord's table, "the breaking of bread," was central to New Testament worship. It pictured worship that is intimate, participatory and Christ-centered. Although every church will need to work through the issue of worship style, we must keep the focus on the object of worship — not merely the style.

Spirit-empowered Prayer. Spirit-filled churches make prayer a central and meaningful part of all that's done. They turn prayer meetings into God meetings, asking the Lord for a growing confidence in his goodness, faithfulness and sufficiency. Something powerful happens to a church when the Holy Spirit bestows a spirit of believing prayer.

The devotions described in verse 42 shaped the contagious faith and winsome spirit pictured in verses 43 to 47. Who wouldn't want to be part of a church characterized by:

- A sense of awe
- Powerful answers to prayer
- A united and loving fellowship
- Unselfish generosity
- Intimate worship
- Glad and sincere hearts
- A spirit of God-directed praise
- A favorable reputation in the community

It was this winsome spirit and contagious faith the Lord used to draw people to Christ. Can you imagine what it must have been like to see people come to faith and join the church on an everyday basis? May the Holy Spirit give us an increasing vision of what he might do in and through us. May he capture our hearts and reshape our devotions.

Day One

Devoted to apostolic teaching

They devoted themselves to the apostles' teaching… (Acts 2:42).

Every day people gathered in the temple courts as the apostles taught seekers and believers alike. All across Jerusalem small groups met in houses to study, worship and break bread together. I don't picture them coming late and sitting in the back — do you? I picture an eagerness to know Christ and to walk in his ways. Don't you love to step into churches where the front rows fill up first and the leaders can't start small-group Bible studies fast enough to meet demand?

Such was the ethos of the early church — not because the apostles were great preachers, but because the people were devoted to their teaching. What was apostolic teaching like? We have a window into the apostles' teaching by studying their messages recorded in Acts, as well as their written teachings that make up the rest of the New Testament. Several characteristics of apostolic teaching stand out when you study the New Testament.

Apostolic teaching is:

- **Christ-centered teaching.** It goes beyond biblical principles and life applications to the centrality of Christ living and reigning in our lives. Paul put it like this:
  We proclaim him, admonishing and teaching everyone with all wisdom, so that we may present everyone perfect in Christ (Colossians 1:28).

- **Life-related teaching.** Most of the New Testament was written in response to people's problems, questions, failures and struggles. Like Jesus, the apostles began with people's felt needs and then directed them to their greatest need — a life that glorifies and enjoys God forever.

- **Doctrinal teaching.** The apostles believed theology (God's unchanging truths) mattered. When you read their epistles, you find teaching that based life applications on clearly articulated doctrinal truths. They taught truth, corrected error and contended with false teachers. Paul instructed Timothy in this way:

  Preach the Word; be prepared in season and out of season; correct, rebuke and encourage — with great patience and careful instruction. For the time will come when men will not put up with sound doctrine (2 Timothy 4:2-3).

- **Biblical teaching.** When you read Paul telling Timothy to "preach the Word," you hear the apostolic conviction that God has revealed himself in the Scriptures. Peter underscored the authority of Scripture with this admonition:

  Above all, you must understand that no prophecy of Scripture came about by the prophet's own interpretation. For prophecy never had its origin in the will of man, but men spoke from God as they were carried along by the Holy Spirit (2 Peter 1:20-21).

Being devoted to apostolic teaching goes beyond what happens in the pulpit. Mostly it is about you and me and our life responses to God's Word. It is about our conviction, passion and devotion to knowing and following Christ.

Conviction. Is the Holy Spirit giving us a growing confidence in the truthfulness of God's Word? Are we coming to Scripture with a teachable spirit that desires to align our attitudes, affections and actions with the commands of Christ? ***What did Paul warn Timothy about in 2 Timothy 4:3-4?*** _____

_____

_____

Passion. Is the Holy Spirit increasing our desire to know Christ better and to follow him more faithfully? Are we experiencing a growing love for his Word and a greater joy in following in his ways? Psalm 119 beautifully expresses the longings of a heart set on God's Word. ***Meditate on Psalm 119:10-16 and then express your desire to know and follow God's Word with greater passion.*** _____

_____

_____

Devotion. Is the Holy Spirit empowering us to study God's Word and put it into practice as a daily way of life? When it comes to knowing and growing in truth, are we becoming more disciplined or less disciplined? Do the people who know us best see our lives being changed by Christ's commands? ***Study 1 John 2:3-6 and put in your own words what is being taught.*** _____

_____

_____

3For the time will come when men will not put up with sound doctrine. Instead, to suit their own desires, they will gather around them a great number of teachers to say what their itching ears want to hear. 4They will turn their ears away from the truth and turn aside to myths.

— 2 Timothy 4:3-4

10I seek you with all my heart; do not let me stray from your commands. 11I have hidden your word in my heart that I might not sin against you. 12Praise be to you, O LORD; teach me your decrees. 13With my lips I recount all the laws that come from your mouth. 14I rejoice in following your statutes as one rejoices in great riches. 15I meditate on your precepts and consider your ways. 16I delight in your decrees; I will not neglect your word.

— Psalm 119:10-16

3We know that we have come to know him if we obey his commands. 4The man who says, "I know him," but does not do what he commands is a liar, and the truth is not in him. 5But if anyone obeys his word, God's love is truly made complete in him. This is how we know we are in him: 6Whoever claims to live in him must walk as Jesus did.   — 1 John 2:3-6

Conclude today's study by asking the Holy Spirit to fill you with greater conviction and passion for his Word, so that you might devote yourself to apostolic teaching. *Identify one action you need to take to strengthen your devotion to God's Word.*_____

_____

_____

_____

Day Two

Devoted to caring fellowship

They devoted themselves to…the fellowship (Acts 2:42).

All the believers were together and had everything in common. Selling their possessions and goods, they gave to anyone as he had need. Every day they continued to meet together in the temple courts. They broke bread in their homes and ate together with glad and sincere hearts…(Acts 2:44-46).

A Spirit-filled church is marked by members who devote themselves to "the fellowship." Being devoted to caring fellowship begins with a conviction that Christ calls us to love his church as he loves his church. He laid down his life for us, and now we are called to lay down our lives for each other. Only the Holy Spirit can give us Christ's love for his people. Most of us have been hurt by Christians and disappointed by churches. Apart from the Holy Spirit, the temptation to give up on the church can be overwhelming. Spirit-given devotion enables us to work through our differences and disappointments with honesty and grace. Such devotion displays Christ's living, reigning presence in our midst.

Study Romans 12:9-18 and list specific instructions about devoting ourselves to the fellowship:

1. _____

2. _____

3. _____

4. _____

5. _____

6. _____

7. _____

8. _____

9. _____

10. _____

⁹Love must be sincere. Hate what is evil; cling to what is good. ¹⁰Be devoted to one another in brotherly love. Honor one another above yourselves. ¹¹Never be lacking in zeal, but keep your spiritual fervor, serving the Lord. ¹²Be joyful in hope, patient in affliction, faithful in prayer. ¹³Share with God's people who are in need. Practice hospitality.

¹⁴Bless those who persecute you; bless and do not curse. ¹⁵Rejoice with those who rejoice; mourn with those who mourn. ¹⁶Live in harmony with one another. Do not be proud, but be willing to associate with people of low position. Do not be conceited.

¹⁷Do not repay anyone evil for evil. Be careful to do what is right in the eyes of everybody. ¹⁸If it is possible, as far as it depends on you, live at peace with everyone.

— **Romans 12:9-18**

What is your part in helping your congregation grow in caring fellowship? What do these passages teach about your responsibilities?

Romans 12:4-8 _____

_____

_____

_____

_____

_____

Hebrews 10:24-25 _____

_____

_____

_____

_____

2 Corinthians 9:6-8 _____

_____

_____

_____

_____

How do you need the Holy Spirit to help you grow in devotion to caring fellowship? Be specific. _____

_____

_____

_____

4Just as each of us has one body with many members, and these members do not all have the same function, 5so in Christ we who are many form one body, and each member belongs to all the others. 6We have different gifts, according to the grace given us. If a man's gift is prophesying, let him use it in proportion to his faith. 7If it is serving, let him serve; if it is teaching, let him teach; 8if it is encouraging, let him encourage; if it is contributing to the needs of others, let him give generously; if it is leadership, let him govern diligently; if it is showing mercy, let him do it cheerfully. — **Romans 12:4-8**

24And let us consider how we may spur one another on toward love and good deeds. 25Let us not give up meeting together, as some are in the habit of doing, but let us encourage one another — and all the more as you see the Day approaching.
— **Hebrews 10:24-25**

6Remember this: Whoever sows sparingly will also reap sparingly, and whoever sows generously will also reap generously. 7Each man should give what he has decided in his heart to give, not reluctantly or under compulsion, for God loves a cheerful giver. 8And God is able to make all grace abound to you, so that in all things at all times, having all that you need, you will abound in every good work.
— **2 Corinthians 9:6-8**

Day Three

Devoted to transforming worship

They devoted themselves to… the breaking of bread… (Acts 2:42).

Can you picture the Jerusalem believers gathering in small groups all across the city? They met in homes to encourage each other and to enjoy the Lord in worship. As they gathered, they would eat a meal together. The meal would culminate in a sacred celebration, where Christ was remembered by breaking bread and sharing a common cup. This "breaking of bread" celebration stood at the heart of New Testament worship. To this day the "communion table" stands as a powerful symbol of what it means to worship Christ.

What did Paul teach about the "breaking of bread" celebration in 1 Corinthians 10:16-17 and 11:23-26? _____

_____

_____

_____

Paul went on to warn the church in Corinth not to eat the bread and drink the cup of the Lord in an unworthy manner. He encouraged them to examine themselves so that they might not sin against the body and blood of the Lord. It was a warning against careless and unthinking worship. True worship is meant to be a transforming encounter with Christ. It is both awesome and intimate. We glorify and enjoy an awesome God through an intimate relationship with the Lord Jesus.

It is important to note the Jerusalem church gathered for worship in two different settings. Luke recorded, *"Every day they continued to meet together in the temple courts. They broke bread in their homes…."* The temple courts provided a place where large groups could gather in a "public way." The apostles led daily gatherings where the gospel was proclaimed, the Scriptures taught and prayers offered. It is also likely they worshiped by singing or chanting psalms, hymns and other spiritual songs.

Second, the believers also gathered in homes as smaller groups. In these smaller gatherings they would break bread and minister to each other in singing and words of wisdom, knowledge, encouragement and instruction. No doubt they would also study the Scriptures together. The apostle Paul described healthy small-group worship as a gathering where each one participates in specific ways, but all of it is *"done for the strengthening of the church"* (1 Cor. 14:26).

16Is not the cup of thanksgiving for which we give thanks a participation in the blood of Christ? And is not the bread that we break a participation in the body of Christ? 17Because there is one loaf, we, who are many, are one body, for we all partake of the one loaf.
— 1 Corinthians 10:16-17

23For I received from the Lord what I also passed on to you: The Lord Jesus, on the night he was betrayed, took bread, 24and when he had given thanks, he broke it and said, "This is my body, which is for you; do this in remembrance of me." 25In the same way, after supper he took the cup, saying, "This cup is the new covenant in my blood; do this, whenever you drink it, in remembrance of me." 26For whenever you eat this bread and drink this cup, you proclaim the Lord's death until he comes.
— 1 Corinthians 11:23-26

Reflect for a moment on why large-group worship in the temple courts and small-group worship in homes were both important to the early church. _____

_____

_____

_____

How do you think the church today should use both large-group and small-group gatherings to nurture meaningful worship and fellowship? _____

_____

_____

_____

What do the following passages teach us about transforming worship? _____

Ephesians 5:18-20 _____

_____

_____

Romans 12:1 _____

_____

_____

What did Jesus emphasize about worship in John 4:23-24? _____

_____

_____

_____

18Do not get drunk on wine, which leads to debauchery. Instead, be filled with the Spirit. 19Speak to one another with psalms, hymns and spiritual songs. Sing and make music in your heart to the Lord, 20always giving thanks to God the Father for everything, in the name of our Lord Jesus Christ.
— **Ephesians 5:18-20**

Therefore, I urge you, brothers, in view of God's mercy, to offer your bodies as living sacrifices, holy and pleasing to God—this is your spiritual act of worship.
— **Romans 12:1**

23Yet a time is coming and has now come when the true worshipers will worship the Father in spirit and truth, for they are the kind of worshipers the Father seeks. 24God is spirit, and his worshipers must worship in spirit and in truth. — **John 4:23-24**

When you read about the worship life of the Jerusalem church, two highlights stand out. First you are struck by the consistency of their participation. Luke wrote about all the believers being together and about worship gatherings taking place every day of the week. Their devotion to worship was demonstrated by consistent participation. It is the same for us. Too many Christians are making worship an occasional practice, as opposed to a devoted one. Let me ask you a personal question. Have you established consistent worship practices? Do you make both large-group worship and small-group fellowship a priority on a weekly basis? My purpose in asking is to challenge you to make worship central to the Holy Spirit's work in your life.

Not only are we struck by the consistency of their worship — we can't help but be impressed by the spirit of their worship. Look at the words Luke used to describe the Jerusalem believers as they gathered for fellowship and worship.

How do his descriptive words help us sense the spirit of transforming worship?

"Everyone was filled with awe..." (Acts 2:43). _____

_____

_____

"They broke bread...with glad and sincere hearts..." (Acts 2:46). _____

_____

_____

"...praising God and enjoying the favor of all the people" (Acts 2:47). _____

_____

_____

We worship the Lord in spirit and truth when the Holy Spirit opens our spirits to respond to God. We sense his glorious might and respond with awe. We experience his love and mercy and respond with glad and sincere hearts. We gather in worship with sinners saved by grace and together we praise God. The Holy Spirit transforms us from the inside out by revealing God's glory and enabling us to respond by giving him the worship he is due. As we worship the Lord, we reflect his beauty and bring his winsome spirit into our relationships.

How do you want the Holy Spirit to strengthen your devotion to transforming worship?

_____

_____

_____

Day Four

Devoted to Spirit-empowered prayer

They devoted themselves to… prayer (Acts 2:42).

Here is a fun assignment. Set aside a time when you can read the book of Acts from beginning to end. Use a highlighter to mark every time Luke records God's people coming before the Lord in prayer. You will be stunned by their devotion to prayer. You also will be struck by how powerfully God responded to their prayers. Spirit-filled churches are devoted to Spirit-empowered prayers.

What is Spirit-empowered prayer? It is prayer guided by the Holy Spirit. Study the following passages and reflect on what it means to pray in the Spirit:

Ephesians 6:18 _____

_____

_____

_____

Romans 8:26-27 _____

_____

_____

_____

_____

Did you notice in Romans 8:27 how the Holy Spirit helps bring our prayers into alignment with God's will?

Praying in the Spirit stands in contrast to praying in the flesh — praying out of desires that are not in accordance with God's will. ***What did the apostle James teach about this in James 4:1-3?*** _____

_____

_____

_____

Give one practical example of how the Holy Spirit led you to pray in accordance with God's will instead of self-centered desires. _____

_____

_____

And pray in the Spirit on all occasions with all kinds of prayers and requests. With this in mind, be alert and always keep on praying for all the saints. — **Ephesians 6:18**

26In the same way, the Spirit helps us in our weakness. We do not know what we ought to pray for, but the Spirit himself intercedes for us with groans that words cannot express. 27And he who searches our hearts knows the mind of the Spirit, because the Spirit intercedes for the saints in accordance with God's will.
— **Romans 8:26-27**

1What causes fights and quarrels among you? Don't they come from your desires that battle within you? 2You want something but don't get it. You kill and covet, but you cannot have what you want. You quarrel and fight. You do not have, because you do not ask God. 3When you ask, you do not receive, because you ask with wrong motives, that you may spend what you get on your pleasures.
— **James 4:1-3**

7If you remain in me and my words remain in you, ask whatever you wish, and it will be given you. 8This is to my Father's glory, that you bear much fruit, showing your-selves to be my disciples.
— **John 15:7-8**

12My command is this: Love each other as I have loved you. 13Greater love has no one than this, that he lay down his life for his friends. 14You are my friends if you do what I command. 15I no longer call you servants, because a servant does not know his master's business. Instead, I have called you friends, for everything that I learned from my Father I have made known to you. 16You did not choose me, but I chose you and appointed you to go and bear fruit—fruit that will last. Then the Father will give you whatever you ask in my name. 17This is my command: Love each other. — **John 15:12-17**

So how do we gain the guidance of the Holy Spirit to pray according to God's will? Jesus taught that effective prayer comes when we are in a right relationship with him, his truth and with each other. *Study John 15:7-8 and 12-17. What promises did he give about prayer in verses 7 and 16?* _____

_____

_____

_____

_____

If we are to pray effectively, how should we be related to…
… Christ? John 15:7 _____

_____

_____

_____

… Christ's words, his truth? John 15:7 _____

_____

_____

_____

… each other as his disciples? John 15:12-17 _____

_____

_____

_____

It makes sense, doesn't it? The Holy Spirit has great freedom to guide our prayers when we abide in Christ, his words abide in us, and we pray out of love for each other.

This is also why praying together makes so much sense. When we pray with other disciples, as they did in the Jerusalem church, we help each other pray in the Spirit. We help each other move beyond prayers that are weak and selfish to prayers that reflect Christ's love and truth. The Holy Spirit delights in bringing believers into loving unity as they seek God's will and work together.

Spirit-empowered prayer is not only Spirit-led, it is "believing prayer." The Holy Spirit gives us the ability to come before the Lord with a spirit of expectation. We come believing God chooses to do his work in response to the prayers of his people. We come believing every prayer is meant to have an answer. We come expecting the Lord to accomplish his purposes because we have come in faith to him.

How does Jesus encourage us to pray believing prayers in Matthew 7:7-11? _____

_____

_____

_____

What does Hebrews 11:6 teach us about believing prayers? _____

_____

_____

_____

How does the Spirit of God empower our prayers? He prompts and guides us to pray in God's will, and he gives us the faith to pray believing prayers. This is why we persevere in prayer instead of giving up when prayers are not quickly answered. As we persist in prayer we continue to seek the Spirit's leading and empowerment. Our prevailing prayers open a door for him to shape our desires and direct our faith. In many ways, prayer is the ultimate spiritual journey.

Describe an experience in your life when God's Spirit used prayer to work in your heart.

_____

_____

_____

_____

_____

_____

_____

7"Ask and it will be given to you; seek and you will find; knock and the door will be opened to you. 8For everyone who asks receives; he who seeks finds; and to him who knocks, the door will be opened. 9Which of you, if his son asks for bread, will give him a stone? 10Or if he asks for a fish, will give him a snake? 11If you, then, though you are evil, know how to give good gifts to your children, how much more will your Father in heaven give good gifts to those who ask him!"   — Matthew 7:7-11

And without faith it is impossible to please God, because anyone who comes to him must believe that he exists and that he rewards those who earnestly seek him.
    — Hebrews 11:6

Day Five

A winsome dynamic

42They devoted themselves to the apostles' teaching and to the fellowship, to the breaking of bread and to prayer. 43Everyone was filled with awe, and many wonders and miraculous signs were done by the apostles. 44All the believers were together and had everything in common. 45Selling their possessions and goods, they gave to anyone as he had need. 46Every day they continued to meet together in the temple courts. They broke bread in their homes and ate together with glad and sincere hearts, 47praising God and enjoying the favor of all the people. And the Lord added to their number daily those who were being saved.

— **Acts 2:42-47**

We must remember that Christ has given us his Spirit to empower our witness. Spirit-filled churches do not exist for themselves. They exist to advance Christ's reign. The four devotions of the Acts church created a winsome dynamic. We are told they *"enjoyed the favor of all the people. And the Lord added to their number daily those who were being saved"* (Acts 2:47).

Study Acts 2:42-47 and describe what made the faith of the Jerusalem church so attractive and contagious to unbelievers. _____

_____

_____

_____

Here is the fact of the matter: Winsome churches not only win some — they win many. Now think about your life and the church to which you belong. How does the Holy Spirit want to work through you and your fellow church members to attract people to Christ? *To what extent are the following characteristics of the Jerusalem church true of your congregation?*

- *A sense of awe:* _____

- *Powerful answers to prayer:* _____

- *A united and loving fellowship:* _____

- *Unselfish generosity:* _____

- *Intimate worship:* _____

- *Glad and sincere hearts:* _____

- *A spirit of God-directed praise:* _____

- *A favorable reputation in the communiy:* _____

Spirit-filled churches are central to Christ's global mission. Churches marked by godly devotion and a winsome dynamic naturally reproduce the life of Christ from person to person and place to place. *Write a prayer expressing how you would like Christ to use you to help raise up a congregation that is increasingly Spirit-filled.* _____

_____

_____

_____

_____

What is our
Guiding Conviction?

Christ is expanding his reign by raising up and reproducing Spirit-filled churches.

For Group Discussion

1. What is the difference between passion and devotion? To what was pastor Craig Bex (in Knoxville, Iowa) truly devoted? To what are you devoted?

2. Which of the four devotions of the Jerusalem church do we do best in our church? As a church, have we minimized or omitted any of the four devotions of the Jerusalem church?

3. Jerry Sheveland describes the eagerness of people in the early church to hear and follow the apostles' teaching. (Day One) Describe how well our devotion to biblical teaching is making us more like Jesus?

4. What do you think of Jerry Sheveland's distinction between devotion to fellowship and being devoted to *the* fellowship? List some ways our caring fellowship is displaying Christ's love to our community.

5. Worship can be a touchy subject because we all have our preferences, prejudices and expectations of what it should be. Evaluate the degree to which visitors sense our church is captivated by the glory of God.

6. For what do we pray expectantly? Name some ways our church has seen prayer bring God's power to bear on the hurts and needs of people in our community.

7. Assess how well the devotions of our church translate into a "winsome dynamic" that impacts our community.

PRAYER POINT • Praise God for his awesome power and glory. Ask God to make our small group an example of "the fellowship" at its very best.

Lesson Five

Delivering His Message

When Peter saw this, he said to them: "Men of Israel, why does this surprise you? Why do you stare at us as if by our own power or godliness we had made this man walk? 13The God of Abraham, Isaac and Jacob, the God of our fathers, has glorified his servant Jesus. You handed him over to be killed, and you disowned him before Pilate, though he had decided to let him go. 14You disowned the Holy and Righteous One and asked that a murderer be released to you. 15You killed the author of life, but God raised him from the dead. We are witnesses of this. 16By faith in the name of Jesus, this man whom you see and know was made strong. It is Jesus' name and the faith that comes through him that has given this complete healing to him, as you can all see.

17"Now, brothers, I know that you acted in ignorance, as did your leaders. 18But this is how God fulfilled what he had foretold through all the prophets, saying that his Christ would suffer. 19Repent, then, and turn to God, so that your sins may be wiped out, that times of refreshing may come from the Lord, 20and that he may send the Christ, who has been appointed for you— even Jesus. 21He must remain in heaven until the time comes for God to restore everything, as he promised long ago through his holy prophets.

Acts 3:12-21

Have you ever had someone ask you an odd question? It happened to me one Sunday morning several years ago. I was pastoring College Avenue Baptist Church in San Diego, Calif. It was the last service of the morning. I had already preached five times and I was weary. A visitor approached me with a request to talk in private. He was the kind of person who stood too close and established eye contact that felt a bit too intense. Quite honestly, I felt a little uncomfortable with the guy. Once we were in my office, he said,

"I have a question from God for you. Are you a messenger of the Lord?" Not sure what he had in mind, I replied, "Well, I have been called to be a pastor and a preacher." The man responded with a second question, "If you are the Lord's messenger, what message has he given you to deliver?"

I had no idea what answer this individual was attempting to get out of me. I just wanted to end the conversation and go home. Then in the middle of my impatience a thought occurred to me. This was not a hard question to answer. I didn't know what he had in mind, but I knew without a doubt the message God has called me to deliver. I preach and teach hundreds of times every year on dozens of different topics, but it all comes down to one central message: Jesus Christ, God's Son and our Savior, crucified, risen and coming again!

- I can't teach about marriage without talking about Christ and his bride, the church. Every other relationship is secondary to our relationship with him.

- Nor can I preach about overcoming stress without offering the invitation of Jesus, *"Come to me all of you who are weary and burdened, and I will give you rest."*

- It's not possible to teach about success in life without giving Christ's warning, *"What does it profit a man to gain the whole world and lose his own soul?"* and then to extend his call, *"Take up your cross and follow me."*

- When it comes to talking about finding peace in life, it is not enough to give people principles of peace when they really need the Prince of Peace.

- Why would I preach about steps to take, or keys to unlock, or secrets to discover, or disciplines to practice without making the greatest mystery of life crystal clear, *"which is Christ in you, the hope of glory"?*

> *Spirit-filled churches have a message to deliver: the gospel of Jesus Christ.*

Each of us has been given the Holy Spirit so that we might bear witness to Christ and his message, the gospel. It is essential, then, for each of us to understand and articulate his message. This is where the third chapter of Acts is so helpful to us. Peter and John were used by the Lord to heal a man crippled from birth. The miracle attracted a crowd of astonished people. Peter took the opportunity to proclaim the gospel — a word that literally means "good news."

Luke gives us a summary of Peter's message. He gives us the key points. Peter began by explaining that the miracle the people witnessed was not about Peter or John.
Men of Israel, why does this surprise you? Why do you stare at us as if by our own power or godliness we had made these men walk (Acts 1:12)?

He refocused the listeners' attention to God's purposes and the power of believing in the name of Jesus. He was saying, in essence, the good news that surrounds this miracle is not about us. It is about the eternal plan of God in Jesus Christ.

On one occasion Dr. Billy Graham decided to preach the same message to two very different audiences. He had preached a simple gospel message from John 3:16 in a remote village setting in Africa. A few weeks later he delivered the same sermon at Oxford University to a gathering of students and professors. The gospel he proclaimed was powerfully used by the Holy Spirit in both places. Like Peter, Dr. Graham trusted the power of the gospel message. It is a good news message about:

- the gracious plan of God
- the guilt of people in need of a savior
- the glory of Christ and his saving work
- the gift of saving faith
- and the great hope of the believer

Day One

The gospel is about the gracious plan of God

The God of Abraham, Isaac and Jacob, the God of our Fathers has glorified his servant Jesus… (Acts 1:13).

Peter wanted his Jewish listeners to understand that the God of their fathers is the same God who anointed Jesus to be their Savior and Christ. Peter concluded his message by explaining that all the prophets of the Old Testament foretold God's eternal plan in Jesus Christ.

Indeed, all the prophets from Samuel on, as many as have spoken, have foretold these days. And you are heirs of the prophets and of the covenant God made with your fathers. He said to Abraham, 'Through your offspring all peoples on earth will be blessed.' When God raised up his servant, he sent him first to you to bless you by turning each of you from your wicked ways (Acts 3:24-26).

The gospel begins with the God of the Ages, who by sovereign grace determined to send Christ to save his people from their wicked ways. Jesus was not an afterthought or a secondary plan. He is the fulfillment of God's gracious plan from all eternity.

How did Peter use the example of Moses to make this point in Acts 3:22-25? _____

_____

_____

_____

In Acts 2:25-31, how did Peter use the example of David to prove his point that Jesus has always been central to God's plan? _____

_____

_____

_____

22"For Moses said, 'The Lord your God will raise up for you a prophet like me from among your own people; you must listen to everything he tells you. 23Anyone who does not listen to him will be completely cut off from among his people.'

24"Indeed, all the prophets from Samuel on, as many as have spoken, have foretold these days. 25And you are heirs of the prophets and of the covenant God made with your fathers. He said to Abraham, 'Through your offspring all peoples on earth will be blessed.'"

–Acts 3:22-25

25"David said about him:
'I saw the Lord always before me.
Because he is at my right hand,
I will not be shaken.
26Therefore my heart is glad and my tongue rejoices;
my body also will live in hope,
27because you will not abandon me to the grave,
nor will you let your Holy One see decay.
28You have made known to me the paths of life;
you will fill me with joy in your presence.'
29"Brothers, I can tell you confidently that the patriarch David died and was buried, and his tomb is here to this day. 30But he was a prophet and knew that God had promised him on oath that he would place one of his descendants on his throne. 31Seeing what was ahead, he spoke of the resurrection of the Christ, that he was not abandoned to the grave, nor did his body see decay."

—Acts 2:25-31

Why do you think it is important to understand that sending Christ has been God's plan from the beginning? _____

_____

_____

Have you ever put a jigsaw puzzle together? If you have, you know every piece has its place in the big picture. So it is with every truth in the Bible. Every story, every psalm, every proverb, every prophecy, every instruction has its place within the big picture. The big picture is God's gracious plan in Jesus Christ.

When I put together a jigsaw puzzle I begin by looking for the pieces with flat sides, because they form the borders. When I put the four borders together, it is easier to put the other pieces in their place. In a similar way there are four great borders that frame the big picture of God's plan. They are:

- **Creation** — God's good design. He created all things for his glory.

- **Fall** — Sin corrupts God's good design and separates sinful people from their Creator.

- **Redemption** — God sends his Son to atone for sin and to reconcile fallen people to himself.

- **Completion** — God's Son restores all things to the Father for his glory's sake.

All Scripture, from Genesis to Revelation, tells this story. The gospel is about God's gracious plan in Jesus Christ. *What should be our response to God when we understand that he has graciously chosen to give us mercy through his Son?* _____

_____

_____

Day Two

The gospel is about the guilt of people in need of a savior

Peter did not spare the feelings of his listeners when he declared they were disowning the very one God had sent to be their Savior and Lord.

The God of Abraham, Isaac and Jacob, the God of our fathers, has glorified his servant Jesus. You handed him over to be killed, and you disowned him before Pilate, though he had decided to let him go. You disowned the Holy and Righteous One and asked that a murderer be released to you. You killed the author of life, but God raised him from the dead. We are witnesses of this (Acts 3:13-15).

What convicting words! People who were already guilty of breaking God's laws and rebelling against his reign disowned the very Savior the Father had sent and handed him over to be killed. Can you imagine the double guilt of needing a savior to deliver you from your sins against God and then disowning the very savior God provides? We can't point our fingers at the Jews in Jerusalem. It is our double guilt as well unless we turn in faith to Jesus Christ.

How did Peter and the other apostles answer the high priest when he accused them of preaching a message of guilt? Acts 5:27-32. _____

_____

_____

_____

What does Romans 3:21-24 teach about our guilt and our need of a savior? _____

_____

_____

_____

_____

Notice that Peter recognized the ignorance of the Jews in Jerusalem at the time when they crucified Jesus. He said, *"Now, brothers, I know that you acted in ignorance, as did your leaders"* (Acts 3:17). He went on to explain that the death of Jesus fulfilled the prophecy that Christ would suffer. He then called them to repent.

Ignorant or not, they were guilty and needed the forgiveness Jesus made possible on the cross. Many today do not feel guilty. They feel they're good people who have made a few mistakes. After all, nobody is perfect. Professional baseball star Pete Rose was banned from the game because of his gambling. He put it like this: "I am not a bad person. I just did some bad things."

27Having brought the apostles, they made them appear before the Sanhedrin to be questioned by the high priest. 28"We gave you strict orders not to teach in this name," he said. "Yet you have filled Jerusalem with your teaching and are determined to make us guilty of this man's blood."

29Peter and the other apostles replied: "We must obey God rather than men! 30The God of our fathers raised Jesus from the dead—whom you had killed by hanging him on a tree. 31God exalted him to his own right hand as Prince and Savior that he might give repentance and forgiveness of sins to Israel. 32We are witnesses of these things, and so is the Holy Spirit, whom God has given to those who obey him."
—Acts 5:27-32

21But now a righteousness from God, apart from law, has been made known, to which the Law and the Prophets testify. 22This righteousness from God comes through faith in Jesus Christ to all who believe. There is no difference, 23for all have sinned and fall short of the glory of God, 24and are justified freely by his grace through the redemption that came by Christ Jesus.
—Romans 3:21-24

Whether we feel guilty is not the issue. We are guilty of breaking God's laws. And we are doubly guilty when we reject the Christ he sent to save us.

Suppose you commit a felony and stand before a judge. He doesn't care if you feel guilty. His judgment is based on your being guilty.

Close today's study by writing a prayer confessing your guilt and need for a savior.

_____

_____

_____

_____

Day Three

The gospel is about the glory of Christ and his saving work

Peter delineated what was at stake. When it comes to Jesus, we either disown him or turn to him, trusting who he is and what he has done for us. Notice how Peter exalted the glory of Christ's name. He spoke of him as:

- the servant God glorified (verse 13)
- the Holy and Righteous One (verse 14)
- the author of life (verse 15)

When Peter spoke about faith in the name of Jesus, he was calling his listeners to believe Jesus is all he claimed to be. To revere him as their Holy and Righteous One and the author of life was to affirm Jesus is the Christ, the divine Son of God. It affirms Jesus — the sinless Son of God — has the rightful authority to save us from our sins.

*What did Peter teach about the name of Jesus in Acts 4:8-12?*_____

_____

_____

_____

_____

8Then Peter, filled with the Holy Spirit, said to them: "Rulers and elders of the people! 9If we are being called to account today for an act of kindness shown to a cripple and are asked how he was healed, 10then know this, you and all the people of Israel: It is by the name of Jesus Christ of Nazareth, whom you crucified but whom God raised from the dead, that this man stands before you healed. 11He is 'the stone you builders rejected, which has become the capstone.' 12Salvation is found in no one else, for there is no other name under heaven given to men by which we must be saved." —Acts 4:8-12

The glory of Christ, however, goes beyond his name to his saving work — his suffering on the cross and his resurrection from the dead. Peter explained it this way:

You killed the author of life, but God raised him from the dead. We are witnesses of this (Acts 3:15).

But this is how God fulfilled what he had foretold through all the prophets, saying that his Christ would suffer (Acts 3:18).

Please feel the power of this truth. The Holy and Righteous One was killed by the sinners he came to save. The author of life died at the hands of the very ones who needed his eternal life. Then God raised him from the dead so that we who deserve death might live. Can you imagine a more glorious or gracious sacrifice?

Look at how Paul described Christ's saving work in Romans 5:6-10. What did he teach?

_____

_____

_____

*How did Paul summarize the gospel of Christ in 1 Corinthians 15:1-4?*_____

_____

_____

_____

Now put the good news about Jesus into your own words. Who is he and what did he do for you? _____

_____

_____

_____

_____

_____

_____

6You see, at just the right time, when we were still powerless, Christ died for the ungodly. 7Very rarely will anyone die for a righteous man, though for a good man someone might possibly dare to die. 8But God demonstrates his own love for us in this: While we were still sinners, Christ died for us.

9Since we have now been justified by his blood, how much more shall we be saved from God's wrath through him! 10For if, when we were God's enemies, we were reconciled to him through the death of his Son, how much more, having been reconciled, shall we be saved through his life! —**Romans 5:6-10**

1Now, brothers, I want to remind you of the gospel I preached to you, which you received and on which you have taken your stand. 2By this gospel you are saved, if you hold firmly to the word I preached to you. Otherwise, you have believed in vain.

3For what I received I passed on to you as of first importance: that Christ died for our sins according to the Scriptures, 4that he was buried, that he was raised on the third day according to the Scriptures....

. —**1 Corinthians 15:1-4**

Day Four

The gospel is about the gift of saving faith

Peter called his listeners to turn from their guilt and put their faith in the name of Jesus. He explained saving faith by pointing to the man who had been healed.

By faith in the name of Jesus, this man whom you see and know was made strong. It is Jesus' name and the faith that comes through him that has given this complete healing to him, as you can all see (Acts 3:16).

Peter underscored two truths about the healed man's faith. First, it was faith in the name of Jesus. He trusted that Jesus was who he claimed to be and that he had the authority to save the man from his condition. Second, Peter asserted that his faith came "through Jesus." Saving faith is a gift. Jesus has done all that is needed for our salvation. He even gives us the ability to believe in him.

Here is how Peter invited the people of Jerusalem to put their faith in Christ.

Repent, then, and turn to God, so that your sins may be wiped out, that times of refreshing may come from the Lord, and that he may send the Christ, who has been appointed for you — even Jesus (Acts 3:19-20).

To repent is to turn in faith from the guilt of our sins to God's provision — Jesus Christ, who suffered and died for our sins and rose again to give us his eternal life. Repentance is a change of mind, turning from disowning Jesus to owning him as Savior and Lord.

How did Jesus explain saving faith in John 3:16-18? _____

_____

_____

_____

_____

How did Paul emphasize that saving faith is a gift of God's grace in Ephesians 2:4-8?

_____

_____

_____

_____

Describe in your own words what it means to turn to Christ in saving faith. _____

_____

_____

_____

16"For God so loved the world that he gave his one and only Son, that whoever believes in him shall not perish but have eternal life. 17For God did not send his Son into the world to condemn the world, but to save the world through him. 18Whoever believes in him is not condemned, but whoever does not believe stands condemned already because he has not believed in the name of God's one and only Son."
—**John 3:16-18**

4But because of his great love for us, God, who is rich in mercy, 5made us alive with Christ even when we were dead in transgressions—it is by grace you have been saved. 6And God raised us up with Christ and seated us with him in the heavenly realms in Christ Jesus, 7in order that in the coming ages he might show the incomparable riches of his grace, expressed in his kindness to us in Christ Jesus. 8For it is by grace you have been saved, through faith— and this not from yourselves, it is the gift of God....
—**Ephesians 2:4-8**

Day Five

The gospel is about
the great hope of the believers

Repent, then, and turn to God, so that your sins may be wiped out, that times of refreshing may come from the Lord, and that he may send the Christ, who has been appointed for you — even Jesus. He must remain in heaven until the time comes for God to restore everything, as he promised long ago through his holy prophets (Acts 3:19-21).

I am impressed by how simply and clearly Peter explained the good news of Jesus.

- He is God's gracious plan…
  for guilty people in need of a savior.

- He is the glorious Christ who provided salvation…
  for all who believe in his name.

It is good news indeed. Yet for the believer, Peter saved the best news for last. Christ not only saves us from the guilt of our sins, but he gives us a great hope. He gives us the promise of refreshing days to come when Christ returns to restore all things to God.

So what exactly did Peter promise in Acts 3:19-23? What did he promise those who believe…

About our sins in verse 19? _____

_____

_____

About Christ's return in verses 19-21? _____

_____

_____

What is promised those who reject Christ in verse 23? _____

_____

_____

The healing of a crippled man became the opportunity to proclaim that a day of restoration for all things is coming. Jesus is the promised Messiah, who will fulfill every prophecy in the old covenant and will bring the long-awaited refreshing. Those who close their ears to him will be forever cut off from his people. Those who turn to him in faith receive his forgiveness and the hope of his return. They live in anticipation of the day when Christ comes to reign and restore all things for the glory of God. Read how the apostle Paul explained all this:

19"Repent, then, and turn to God, so that your sins may be wiped out, that times of refreshing may come from the Lord, 20and that he may send the Christ, who has been appointed for you — even Jesus. 21He must remain in heaven until the time comes for God to restore everything, as he promised long ago through his holy prophets. 22For Moses said, 'The Lord your God will raise up for you a prophet like me from among your own people; you must listen to everything he tells you. 23Anyone who does not listen to him will be completely cut off from among his people.'"
—**Acts 3:19-23**

13Brothers, we do not want you to be ignorant about those who fall asleep, or to grieve like the rest of men, who have no hope. 14We believe that Jesus died and rose again and so we believe that God will bring with Jesus those who have fallen asleep in him. 15According to the Lord's own word, we tell you that we who are still alive, who are left till the coming of the Lord, will certainly not precede those who have fallen asleep. 16For the Lord himself will come down from heaven, with a loud command, with the voice of the archangel and with the trumpet call of God, and the dead in Christ will rise first. 17After that, we who are still alive and are left will be caught up together with them in the clouds to meet the Lord in the air. And so we will be with the Lord forever. 18Therefore encourage each other with these words.   —1 Thessalonians 4:13-18

5All this is evidence that God's judgment is right, and as a result you will be counted worthy of the kingdom of God, for which you are suffering. 6God is just: He will pay back trouble to those who trouble you 7and give relief to you who are troubled, and to us as well. This will happen when the Lord Jesus is revealed from heaven in blazing fire with his powerful angels. 8He will punish those who do not know God and do not obey the gospel of our Lord Jesus. 9They will be punished with everlasting destruction and shut out from the presence of the Lord and from the majesty of his power 10on the day he comes to be glorified in his holy people and to be marveled at among all those who have believed. This includes you, because you believed our testimony to you.
          —2 Thessalonians 1:5-10

What does 1 Thessalonians 4:13-18 teach us about Christ's return and those who believe?

_____

_____

_____

What does 2 Thessalonians 1:5-10 teach us about Christ's return and those who reject the gospel? _____

_____

_____

The message entrusted to us is one of life-and-death importance. Every one of us must be ready to share it at every opportunity. There are a number of excellent tools you can use to explain the gospel to others. Your church probably recommends a booklet or gospel tract that lays out the gospel in a simple and clear way. Learn to use one of these tools or learn how to share the gospel directly from the Bible.

Be sure to…

- Know the gospel.
- Experience the power of the gospel in your life.
- Practice explaining the gospel until you can share it clearly and naturally.
- Ask the Holy Spirit to use you in bringing the gospel to others.
- Look for and take advantage of every opportunity to deliver the message.

So here is our guiding conviction: Spirit-filled churches have a message to deliver: the gospel of Jesus Christ. Spirit-filled churches not only deliver the gospel — they embody the gospel. They experience and express the gospel in all they do. **What would your church look like if its members were passionate about...**

God's gracious plan in Jesus Christ? _____

_____

_____

The glory of Christ and his saving work? _____

_____

_____

The guilt of sinful people in need of a savior? _____

_____

_____

The gift of saving faith? _____

_____

_____

The great hope that is ours in Christ? _____

_____

_____

What is our
Guiding Conviction?

Spirit-filled
churches
have a message
to deliver:
the gospel of
Jesus Christ.

Has the gospel become old news to you instead of good news? Or is God's gracious provision of Jesus Christ continuing to transform your attitudes, affections and behavior? The gospel is meant to do a deep and continuing work in our lives. As it produces humility, grace, joy, gratitude, holiness and hope in us, our message increasingly rings true in the ears of those who hear us.

For Group Discussion

1. Describe your level of comfort or discomfort with defining the gospel. With explaining it to an unbeliever.

2. Explain why many people today do not feel guilty before God. What is their "double guilt"? (Day Two)

3. List a couple of ways you maintain a fresh, vibrant and motivating appreciation for Christ's sacrifice. How well does your life embody the gospel? (Day Three)

4. Summarize why saving faith can only be received as a gift. (Day Four) Why is self-righteousness absurd behavior for a believer?

5. Evaluate how well our church "experiences and expresses the gospel in all we are and do." How much do visitors sense our delight in receiving undeserved mercy instead of condemnation?

6. Name some tools our church is using to deliver the gospel to unbelievers. What is most helpful to you in sharing your faith?

8. Identify what gives you the greatest joy when you think about Christ's return. (Day Five)

PRAYER POINT • Continue to pray by name for those in our sphere of influence (Lesson Three). Pray for a harvest of new believers in our community. Thank God for hope in Jesus Christ.

Lesson Six

Emboldened by His Courage

The priests and the captain of the temple guard and the Sadducees came up to Peter and John while they were speaking to the people. ²They were greatly disturbed because the apostles were teaching the people and proclaiming in Jesus the resurrection of the dead. ³They seized Peter and John, and because it was evening, they put them in jail until the next day. ⁴But many who heard the message believed, and the number of men grew to about five thousand.

⁵The next day the rulers, elders and teachers of the law met in Jerusalem. ⁶Annas the high priest was there, and so were Caiaphas, John, Alexander and the other men of the high priest's family. ⁷They had Peter and John brought before them and began to question them: "By what power or what name did you do this?"

⁸Then Peter, filled with the Holy Spirit, said to them: "Rulers and elders of the people! ⁹If we are being called to account today for an act of kindness shown to a cripple and are asked how he was healed, ¹⁰then know this, you and all the people of Israel: It is by the name of Jesus Christ of Nazareth, whom you crucified but whom God raised from the dead, that this man stands before you healed. ¹¹He is

"'the stone you builders rejected,
    which has become the capstone.'

¹²Salvation is found in no one else, for there is no other name under heaven given to men by which we must be saved."

¹³When they saw the courage of Peter and John and realized that they were unschooled, ordinary men, they were astonished and they took note that these men had been with Jesus....

²³On their release, Peter and John went back to their own people and reported all that the chief priests and elders had said to them. ²⁴When they heard this, they raised their voices together in prayer to God....

²⁹"Now, Lord, consider their threats and enable your servants to speak your word with great boldness. ³⁰Stretch out your hand to heal and perform miraculous signs and wonders through the name of your holy servant Jesus."

³¹After they prayed, the place where they were meeting was shaken. And they were all filled with the Holy Spirit and spoke the word of God boldly.   **Acts 4:1-13, 23-24, 29-31**

Jerusalem is perched along the largest land rift on the face of the earth. The rift begins in Lebanon and forms the Jordan Valley down through the Dead Sea and on to the Gulf of Aqaba. It shapes the Red Sea and then slashes down the center of East Africa. This great rift is formed by two huge sections of the earth's crust, the African and Arabian plates. These two plates are moving upward and away from each other at about the same pace as your fingernails are growing. The movement creates a springlike tension along fault lines that crisscross the Jordan Valley. The tension builds until ground shifts trigger vibrations to the earth's surface. We call those vibrations earthquakes. There are 400 to 600 earthquakes every year in Israel. Most go unnoticed, but a major earthquake occurs about every 100 years. The last big one was in 1927. The one before that was in 1837.

Why did I give you this little geography lesson? From time to time the Lord has used this unique feature of his creation to signal his presence to his people.

- When the Lord God of Israel was about to deliver the Ten Commandments to Moses, he displayed his awesome holiness before his people by shaking the mountain.
- When Uzziah, the longest-reigning king of Israel, became proud of his great buildings and massive army, God toppled his empire with an earthquake of astonishing proportions. A recent technical report gives evidence that it was the largest earthquake in the last 4000 years of Israel's history.
- The earth shook again when Christ was crucified, tearing the temple curtain.
- Then on Easter morning the earth quaked as the stone was rolled away from the grave of our risen Savior.

The ground beneath Jerusalem shook once more when the church gathered in prayer and asked the Lord to stretch forth his hand and touch their city. Peter and John had been threatened by the authorities to stop speaking in the name of Jesus. When they brought the news to the gathered believers, the church's first response was to pray. They laid claim to God's sovereign purposes and petitioned him for boldness to speak and for a display of his supernatural presence. The Lord responded, and the tremors of his touch shook the room as his Spirit filled them with boldness. He shook his church in order to shake the city and ultimately the world.

When I read this account, I long to pray, "Shake us again, Lord." Shake us that we might...

- Proclaim a bolder witness.
- Pray bolder prayers.
- Practice a bolder faith.

Day One

Shake us again –
until we proclaim a bolder witness

After they prayed, the place where they were meeting was shaken. And they were all filled with the Holy Spirit and spoke the word of God boldly (Acts 4:31).

The word *boldness* has as its root the word *speech*. Its prefix is the word *all*. It carries the idea of not holding back — saying all that needs to be said. It expresses the idea of turning fear into confidence.

What is pictured in this scene is the kind of boldness that flows from humility, not self-confidence. The Jerusalem believers reflected the bold humility and servant obedience of Peter and John, who proclaimed to the rulers and elders:

Judge for yourselves whether it is right in God's sight to obey you rather than God. For we cannot help speaking about what we have seen and heard (Acts 4:19-20).

It is not the kind of boldness we pump up when a high school football team rushes onto the field for the big homecoming game. This is a Spirit-given boldness that strengthens a humble servant even when he or she is exhausted, frazzled and scared spitless. We don't need any more hype and rah-rah in our lives. We need what Peter got. We need what John got. We need the Spirit who shook the Jerusalem church to shake us.

Just the other day my wife Dawn was enjoying a conversation with a woman who is Jewish but not practicing faith of any kind. This bright, successful businesswoman described to Dawn her frustration over the tensions and conflicts in the Middle East. As Dawn listened, she sensed in her spirit that she needed to talk to this woman about Christ. She also felt a growing fear of offending her by talking about Jesus. Dawn gave her fear to the Lord by silently praying, "Father, please don't let me wimp out." God's Spirit answered that quick prayer by giving Dawn the words to share Christ naturally and clearly. The woman listened without responding and then changed the topic of conversation. It was a brief opportunity Dawn stepped into by simply seeking Spirit-given boldness. How the Spirit uses Dawn's witness is up to God and his ongoing work in the woman's life.

Learning to practice boldness is a spiritual growth issue in every believer's life. Like the early church, we can learn from Peter and John's example how to be bold in the face of opposition.

⁵The next day the rulers, elders and teachers of the law met in Jerusalem. ⁶Annas the high priest was there, and so were Caiaphas, John, Alexander and the other men of the high priest's family. ⁷They had Peter and John brought before them and began to question them: "By what power or what name did you do this?"

⁸Then Peter, filled with the Holy Spirit, said to them: "Rulers and elders of the people! ⁹If we are being called to account today for an act of kindness shown to a cripple and are asked how he was healed, ¹⁰then know this, you and all the people of Israel: It is by the name of Jesus Christ of Nazareth, whom you crucified but whom God raised from the dead, that this man stands before you healed. ¹¹He is

"'the stone you builders rejected,
   which has become the capstone.'
¹²Salvation is found in no one else, for there is no other name under heaven given to men by which we must be saved."

¹³When they saw the courage of Peter and John and realized that they were unschooled, ordinary men, they were astonished and they took note that these men had been with Jesus. ¹⁴But since they could not see the man who had been healed standing there with them, there was nothing they could say. ¹⁵So they ordered them to withdraw from the Sanhedrin and then conferred togther. ¹⁶"What are we going to do with these men?" they asked. "Everybody living in Jerusalem knows they have done an outstanding miracle, and we cannot deny it. ¹⁷But to stop this thing from spreading any further among the people, we must warn these men to speak no longer to anyone in this name."

¹⁸Then they called them in again and commanded them not to speak or teach at all in the name of Jesus. ¹⁹But Peter and John replied, "Judge for yourselves whether it is right in God's sight to obey you rather than God. ²⁰For we cannot help speaking about what we have seen and heard."

²¹After further threats they let them go. They could not decide how to punish them, because all the people were praising God for what had happened.   —Acts 4:5-21

Study Acts 4:5-21 and answer the following questions:

How did Peter and John answer the rulers and elders? (verses 8-12) _____

_____

_____

What was it that astonished the religious leaders about Peter and John's boldness? (verse 13) _____

_____

_____

How did they attempt to pressure the apostles into silence about Jesus? (verse 18) _____

_____

_____

How did the apostles answer? (verse 19) _____

_____

_____

When the apostle Paul wrote to Timothy about this issue of boldness, he addressed the issues of fear and embarrassment. Every time I read Paul's admonition, it feels as if it was written just for me. *Read 2 Timothy 1:6-12 and reflect on our need to turn from our timidity to the Holy Spirit's empowerment.*

How does a spirit of timidity and embarrassment hinder our witness? _____

_____

_____

What kind of spirit comes from God? _____

_____

_____

Why did Paul say he was not ashamed to boldly proclaim the gospel? _____

_____

_____

We are not called to be obnoxious or pushy, but we are called to be Christ's witnesses. *What are some steps of boldness you need to take, and how do you need the Holy Spirit's help to take them?* _____

_____

_____

_____

Day Two

Shake us again — until we pray bolder prayers

Now, Lord, consider their threats and enable your servants to speak your word with great boldness. Stretch out your hand to heal and perform miraculous signs and wonders through the name of your holy servant Jesus (Acts 4:29-30).

When I took a second look at this passage, it struck me that proclaiming a bolder witness is a secondary step. Bold witness came as a result of praying bold prayers. So it is with us. We will not proclaim a bolder witness until we pray bolder prayers.

The congregation in Jerusalem didn't pray, "God, you know that Pete and John are good guys who got a bad deal. Please deliver them from this hard place, and let them serve you in peace and safety. Oh, and while you're at it, protect us too. You know we are busy

6For this reason I remind you to fan into flame the gift of God, which is in you through the laying on of my hands. 7For God did not give us a spirit of timidity, but a spirit of power, of love and of self-discipline.

8So do not be ashamed to testify about our Lord, or ashamed of me his prisoner. But join with me in suffering for the gospel, by the power of God, 9who has saved us and called us to a holy life—not because of anything we have done but because of his own purpose and grace. This grace was given us in Christ Jesus before the beginning of time, 10but it has now been revealed through the appearing of our Savior, Christ Jesus, who has destroyed death and has brought life and immortality to light through the gospel. 11And of this gospel I was appointed a herald and an apostle and a teacher. 12That is why I am suffering as I am. Yet I am not ashamed, because I know whom I have believed, and am convinced that he is able to guard what I have entrusted to him for that day. **— 2 Timothy 1:6-12**

people with careers to build, homes to decorate, successful children to raise and lake cabins to visit. We know you love us and want to bless us, so set a hedge of protection around our pleasant, comfortable, well-planned little lives." No! They boldly asked God for three things. First, regarding the threats against them, they said, "It's your business, not ours, how you choose to use this persecution." Second, they said, "Stretch out your hand and touch this city with your miraculous presence." And third, they said, "Enable us to be bold."

I was pastoring a church in Littleton, Colo., when the tragedy at Columbine High School turned our community inside out. The multiple shooting deaths of students and one of their teachers shattered the illusion of a peaceful suburb out of harm's way. I was amazed by how churches and Christians rose up to minister to hurts and needs in the aftermath of the tragedy. In the months prior to the shootings, youth pastors had worked together to establish student-led prayer movements on the various middle school and high school campuses across Littleton. Many churches and pastors had also been involved in various cooperative prayer and ministry efforts directed toward the community. God's Spirit had prepared God's people through united prayer to step into the tragedy and make a difference.

Not long ago I was with a pastor of a small church in rural Illinois. He had felt led to challenge his congregation to pray for 52 people to come to Christ through the influences of the congregation — a person for every week of the year. The Lord honored their prayer goal. Every month they witnessed people turning to Christ. Then on the last week of the year several came to faith, bringing the total to 52. It was a transforming experience for both pastor and congregation.

Spirit-empowered prayer was one of the four devotions that characterized the Jerusalem church. Read the prayer they lifted up to the Lord as they sought his help in the face of opposition. *What impresses you about the prayer Luke recorded in Acts 4:29-30?*

_____

_____

_____

_____

29"Now, Lord, consider their threats and enable your servants to speak your word with great boldness. 30Stretch out your hand to heal and perform miraculous signs and wonders through the name of your holy servant Jesus."
— Acts 4:29-30

Mission America is a wonderful organization that is helping churches across our country raise up "Lighthouses of Prayer." These "Lighthouses of Prayer" are families or other circles of believers who pray together for people in their neighborhood, schools or workplaces who need Christ. Believers are taught how to do three basic tasks as they attempt to be a light–house in their circle of influence. The first task is to identify five individuals in need of Christ. It is a process of asking the Lord for specific people to love and pray for in the name of Jesus. Each of us needs a garden to tend, a circle of friendship with unbelievers.

Stop a moment and begin to identify several unbelievers with whom you could build a relationship — your garden to tend:

1. _____

2. _____

3. _____

4. _____

5. _____

The second task is to pray regularly and specifically for those God puts on your heart. Mission America teaches a simple prayer formula based on the acronym BLESS:

Body – pray for their physical needs

Labor – pray for their employment and work needs

Emotions – pray for their emotional needs

Social – pray for their relational needs

Spiritual – pray for their need for Christ

The third task is to be available to God to bless the people for whom we are praying. The Jerusalem church not only asked God to work in a powerful way — they also asked the Lord to use them and make them bold. As we pray to ask God to bless people, we also ask him to make us a blessing in their lives.

Dawn and I were praying in this way for our next-door neighbors during the time we lived in Littleton, Colo. We lived next door to a husband and wife with two small children. We enjoyed building a friendship with this delightful young family. Tragically, the couple's relationship unraveled and led to a messy divorce. We continued to pray and reach out to both husband and wife. I had the privilege of guiding the young man into a growing relationship with Christ. He lost his marriage but found Jesus in a fresh and deeper way. When we love and pray for people, God will often open the door for us to be a blessing in their lives.

Look at the names you listed above and think about how you might pray for them and be a blessing in their lives. *What practical steps would you need to take to begin investing in their lives?* _____

_____

_____

_____

_____

Day Three

Shake us again —
until we practice a bolder faith

When they heard this, they raised their voices together in prayer to God. "Sovereign Lord," they said, "you made the heaven and the earth and the sea, and everything in them. You spoke by the Holy Spirit through the mouth of your servant, our father David: 'Why do the nations rage and the peoples plot in vain? The kings of the earth take their stand and the rulers gather together against the Lord and against his Anointed One.' Indeed Herod and Pontius Pilate met together with the Gentiles and the people of Israel in this city to conspire against your holy servant Jesus, whom you anointed. They did what your power and will had decided beforehand should happen" (Acts 4:24-28).

A third look at Acts 4 prompted the realization I had this passage backward in my thinking. Bold witness and bold prayers are preceded by a bold vision of God. The Jerusalem church appealed to God as the Sovereign Lord who rules over his creation. They laid hold of a God who is true to his Word. They fixed their faith on the One who had foreseen the conspiracy of the rulers and had chosen to accomplish his will through their actions. He accomplished what he had decided beforehand should happen.

Read Acts 4:24-28 above and jot down how they addressed God and what they believed to be true about him. _____

_____

_____

_____

When the believers lifted up their prayers, they quoted Psalm 2, where David asked, "Why do the nations rage?" The word *rage* comes from the image of high-spirited horses neighing, snorting and stomping the ground.

One Sunday afternoon outside Sioux Falls, S.D., I observed a yearling being broken. Neil Hughes is a pastor who trains cutting horses as a sideline. I watched Neil work with a fiery young horse for the better part of an hour. The yearling snorted and raged, but Neil gently and persistently brought it to a place of submission. It was amazing to watch.

Do we genuinely believe God is Sovereign and capable of bringing all things into submission to his will? Do we genuinely believe Christ when he says, *"All authority in heaven and in earth has been given to me…and surely I am with you always?"* It is our confidence in him that breaks the bonds of fear and sets us free to be bold in prayer and bold in witness.

Read Acts 5:27-32 and describe how the apostles answered the threats of the high priest.

_____

_____

_____

_____

How did their belief in God and their confidence in Christ give them courage?

_____

_____

_____

Here's the picture. Standing like tiny specks on the earth's crust, the nations rage and plot in vain — like unbroken yearlings — against the Sovereign Lord of heaven and earth. His servants, prompted by a bold theology, prayed bold prayers for a bold witness. And God rolled up his sleeves, stretched out his hand and gave a little tug to the edge of the Jordan Rift — shaking his church so that they might shake the world.

Like planet earth as a whole, the Jordan Rift is groaning in anticipation of that great moment of release, when Christ will return with his holy servants. The moment his feet touch the Mount of Olives, the great rift will give one last groan and then break open like childbirth. According to the prophet Zechariah, the valley will split in two. Jerusalem's Golden Gate, now sealed with brick, will break apart, and we shall march at Christ's side as he enters the Holy City. Every raging knee will bow.

What do you personally believe about God that gives you the courage you need to be bold in prayer and witness? _____

_____

_____

_____

27Having brought the apostles, they made them appear before the Sanhedrin to be questioned by the high priest. 28"We gave you strict orders not to teach in this name," he said. "Yet you have filled Jerusalem with your teaching and are determined to make us guilty of this man's blood."

29Peter and the other apostles replied: "We must obey God rather than men! 30The God of our fathers raised Jesus from the dead—whom you had killed by hanging him on a tree. 31God exalted him to his own right hand as Prince and Savior that he might give repentance and forgiveness of sins to Israel. 32We are witnesses of these things, and so is the Holy Spirit, whom God has given to those who obey him."

— Acts 5:27-32

Day Four

'We must obey God'

17Then the high priest and all his associates, who were members of the party of the Sadducees, were filled with jealousy. 18They arrested the apostles and put them in the public jail. 19But during the night an angel of the Lord opened the doors of the jail and brought them out. 20"Go, stand in the temple courts," he said, "and tell the people the full message of this new life."

21At daybreak they entered the temple courts, as they had been told, and began to teach the people.

When the high priest and his associates arrived, they called together the Sanhedrin — the full assembly of the elders of Israel — and sent to the jail for the apostles. 22But on arriving at the jail, the officers did not find them there. So they went back and reported, 23"We found the jail securely locked, with the guards standing at the doors; but when we opened them, we found no one inside." 24On hearing this report, the captain of the temple guard and the chief priests were puzzled, wondering what would come of this.

25Then someone came and said, "Look! The men you put in jail are standing in the temple courts teaching the people." 26At that, the captain went with his officers and brought the apostles. They did not use force, because they feared that the people would stone them.

27Having brought the apostles, they made them appear before the Sanhedrin to be questioned by the high priest. 28"We gave you strict orders not to teach in this name," he said. "Yet you have filled Jerusalem with your teaching and are determined to make us guilty of this man's blood."

29Peter and the other apostles replied: "We must obey God rather than men! 30The God of our fathers raised Jesus from the dead—whom you had killed by hanging him on a tree. 31God exalted him to his own right hand as Prince and Savior that he might give repentance and forgiveness of sins to Israel. 32We are witnesses of these things, and so is the Holy Spirit, whom God has given to those who obey him."   **Acts 5:17-32**

Luke picks up the story of the apostles' courage in Acts 5:17. Their decision to remain bold in speech resulted in a confrontation with the high priest and the Jewish high court — the Sanhedrin. The disciples understood their choice was clear. They would either obey God, or they would obey men. Choosing to please people instead of being faithful to God was not an option for them. *Study Acts 5:17-32 above and reflect on the following questions:*

What motivated the religious leaders to oppose the apostles? See verses 17-18.

_____

_____

How did God work to encourage the disciples in their boldness? See verses 19-24.

_____

_____

How would you have felt if you were threatened before a high court like the apostles were? See verses 25-28. _____

_____

_____

_____

Put in your own words how the apostles answered in verses 29-32. _____

_____

_____

Describe an experience when you needed to choose between pleasing God or pleasing people? _____

_____

_____

When I was 16 years old, I gave my life to the Lord to serve him in any way he desired. Within a few days of making that spiritual decision, I found my commitment tested. A school friend asked me to speak at one of the extracurricular clubs in our high school. He said I could speak on any topic I might choose. Immediately, I knew it was an opportunity to share about Jesus. I also knew it meant obeying God rather than pleasing my fellow students.

We face that same choice of obedience in a hundred different ways as we go through daily life. It is normal to want to please people, and it is healthy not to want to offend others. We are even taught by Paul in Colossians 4:6 to season our witness with words filled with grace. Yet when it comes to sharing Christ boldly, we must obey God over people.

Conclude today's study by being honest about your own "people-pleasing" tendencies, and ask the Lord for help. _____

_____

_____

_____

_____

Day Five

'Suffering disgrace for the Name'

33When they heard this, they were furious and wanted to put them to death. 34But a Pharisee named Gamaliel, a teacher of the law, who was honored by all the people, stood up in the Sanhedrin and ordered that the men be put outside for a little while. 35Then he addressed them: "Men of Israel, consider carefully what you intend to do to these men. 36Some time ago Theudas appeared, claiming to be somebody, and about four hundred men rallied to him. He was killed, all his followers were dispersed, and it all came to nothing. 37After him, Judas the Galilean appeared in the days of the census and led a band of people in revolt. He too was killed, and all his followers were scattered. 38Therefore, in the present case I advise you: Leave these men alone! Let them go! For if their purpose or activity is of human origin, it will fail. 39But if it is from God, you will not be able to stop these men; you will only find yourselves fighting against God."

40His speech persuaded them. They called the apostles in and had them flogged. Then they ordered them not to speak in the name of Jesus, and let them go.

41The apostles left the Sanhedrin, rejoicing because they had been counted worthy of suffering disgrace for the Name. 42Day after day, in the temple courts and from house to house, they never stopped teaching and proclaiming the good news that Jesus is the Christ. **Acts 5:33-42**

One night, years ago, I sat in a one-room grass hut with a small circle of Christian men. We were gathered in the middle of the night because it was illegal for these men to meet for worship. One by one they shared with me how they had come to faith in Christ. As they told their stories, I learned that every man in the room had been imprisoned for following Jesus. We worshiped and prayed in whispers around a single lit candle. They described to me the joy of following Jesus, even though it had meant a prison cell for each of them. I was both humbled and strengthened by their examples.

We feel the same way when we read about the apostles *"rejoicing because they had been counted worthy of suffering disgrace for the Name."* At the core of their boldness was a willingness to suffer. Even in their suffering there was a sense of privilege and joy. Amazing!

Take a close look at Acts 5:33-42 and reflect on the following questions:

What do you think of Gamaliel's words of counsel to the Sanhedrin? See verses 33-39.

_____

_____

*Even though they were persuaded by Gamaliel's appeal, they still flogged and threatened the apostles. Why do you think they did it?*_____

_____

_____

What was the apostles' response? See verses 41-42. _____

_____

_____

What does the apostles' example inspire in your heart? _____

_____

_____

Here was a Spirit-filled church with Spirit-filled leaders that literally filled their city with controversy. Their presence and bold witness in Jerusalem could not be ignored. Can that be said of us? Can it be said of our churches?

Isn't it interesting that their witness was both attractive and repulsive at the same time? They were both a blessing and a disgrace. We are told in Acts 2:47 they *"enjoyed the favor of all the people."* Then we find them accused in Acts 5:28 of filling *"Jerusalem with your teaching"* and determining *"to make us guilty of this man's blood."*

May God save us from being nice churches filled with nice Christians. May he embolden us to stand with the apostles and rejoice in being found worthy of disgrace for the name of Christ.

Lord, will you shake us again? Will you shake us free from small dreams and safe prayers and make us so bold that the people of every raging nation might hear your voice, receive your touch and come to their knees?

So, how about you? What is holding you back from greater boldness? _____

_____

_____

How do you want the Holy Spirit to shake your life and your church? _____

_____

_____

_____

_____

What is our
Guiding Conviction?

Christ is
expanding
his reign
through
Spirit-
emboldened
witnesses.

For Group Discussion

1. Explain what went through your mind when you read these words: "I long to pray, 'Shake us again, Lord.'" Would doing that feel risky to you, or would it be empowering?

2. Describe a time the Holy Spirit enabled you to witness when you felt like "wimping out." (Day One)

3. Tell us what holds you back from greater boldness for God. (Day Five)

4. When it comes to your prayer life, how would you rate yourself:

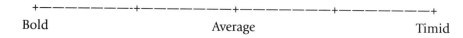

Bold   Average   Timid

5. What do you believe about God that gives you the courage you need to be bold in prayer and witness? (Day Three)

6. How can we get past our fear of offending others when we sense the Spirit prompting us to witness? Which exercises more influence on you: awe at God's greatness or a sense of inadequacy? (Day Four)

7. Describe a time someone you know has suffered for the name of Christ. (Day Five) How do you feel about our church becoming so bold and effective in reaching our community that we attract some people and repulse others?

8. Summarize some steps we can take to become bolder witnesses. What steps might our church take?

PRAYER POINT • Ask God to give us a greater vision of his glory, to strengthen our faith and overcome our inadequacies. Ask him to help us pray with boldness. Let's pray that God would shake us.

Lesson Seven

Purified by His Discipline

Now a man named Ananias, together with his wife Sapphira, also sold a piece of property. ²With his wife's full knowledge he kept back part of the money for himself, but brought the rest and put it at the apostles' feet.

³Then Peter said, "Ananias, how is it that Satan has so filled your heart that you have lied to the Holy Spirit and have kept for yourself some of the money you received for the land? ⁴Didn't it belong to you before it was sold? And after it was sold, wasn't the money at your disposal? What made you think of doing such a thing? You have not lied to men but to God."

⁵When Ananias heard this, he fell down and died. And great fear seized all who heard what had happened. ⁶Then the young men came forward, wrapped up his body, and carried him out and buried him.

⁷About three hours later his wife came in, not knowing what had happened. ⁸Peter asked her, "Tell me, is this the price you and Ananias got for the land?"

"Yes," she said, "that is the price."

⁹Peter said to her, "How could you agree to test the Spirit of the Lord? Look! The feet of the men who buried your husband are at the door, and they will carry you out also."

¹⁰At that moment she fell down at his feet and died. Then the young men came in and, finding her dead, carried her out and buried her beside her husband. ¹¹Great fear seized the whole church and all who heard about these events.

Acts 5:1-11

When you hear the term "deadly virus," what comes to mind? You might immediately think about HIV/AIDS, where sickness and death are passed from life to life. Or you might picture a computer bug worming its way into your software and information files, corrupting and destroying everything it touches. In the fifth chapter of Acts, a very different image of a deadly virus is depicted through the hypocrisy of a couple named Ananias and Sapphira.

The story of this couple's hidden sin is contrasted with the sincere generosity of Barnabas, as described in Acts 4:32-37. He sold a field and gave the money to the church. Barnabas' gift came from a big-hearted desire to care for and encourage others. Barnabas, like so many in the early church, lived out a faith that was genuine and authentic. He was the real deal.

We are told in Acts 2:46 that the Jerusalem believers were characterized by "glad and sincere hearts." It was one of the reasons they enjoyed the favor of those who observed their lives. Authentic faith is infectious. Following Christ with sincere motives is one of the great hallmarks of a Spirit-filled church.

As I write these words, a conversation from last evening immediately comes to mind. My wife Dawn and I attended a worship service packed with young adults. All the chairs in the room were filled, and hundreds more sat on the floor. The energy in the room was electric. After the service we talked with a newly married couple. They told us about a Bible study they host in their home for seekers and new believers. This couple radiated a spirit of innocent joy that captured our hearts.

What a tragedy when sincere faith is replaced by the appearance of spirituality. It is for this reason that hypocrisy is so deadly in the life of a believer and in the fellowship of a church.

We are told in Acts 5:1-11 Ananias and Sapphira sold some property and gave part of the proceeds to the church. From the standpoint of outward appearances, their generous act was no different from that of Barnabas' gift. They were free to give as much or as little as they might choose. Their sin was a hidden one. They gave the impression they were giving all the proceeds from the sale, when in truth they held back part of the money for themselves.

Peter confronted the hidden sin by explaining it was an act of spiritual deception. Look at how Peter describes their hypocrisy:

> …*how is it that Satan has filled your heart that you have lied to the Holy Spirit…. What made you think of doing such a thing? You have not lied to men but to God* (Acts 5:3,4).

God acted decisively to protect his church. He struck down both husband and wife. A sense of fear fell over the church. God had made his point. Hypocrisy is a deadly virus. It must be resisted by all who cherish authentic faith.

The deception of Ananias and Sapphira was dangerous for several reasons.

- Whenever we focus on external appearances instead of sincere motives, we are vulnerable to spiritual deception. We can end up living two lives. Our public self that others see can become very different from the private self seen by God. In short, our very lives can become a lie.

- More important, the hypocrisy of hidden sins and false motives is a lie against the Holy Spirit. When we stop being honest with God about our choices and motives, we test his Holy Spirit. We are saying, "I can continue in hidden sin and still experience the power of the Holy Spirit in my life." It is a lie.

Spirit-filled churches nurture and guard faith that springs from sincere hearts.

- In addition, our acts of hypocrisy hurt the church. We allow the devil to attack the health of our fellowship by filling our hearts with deception instead of sincerity. We lose the capacity to build up the body by speaking the truth in love.

You see, the real issue is not sin. We all fall short of God's good design and trespass against his laws on a daily basis. The issue is not even making choices that are inconsistent with our professed beliefs. None of us consistently "walk the talk." Because of our sins and inconsistencies, we all need the forgiveness that comes from the cross of Christ. The real issue is harboring hidden sins while giving the appearance of spiritual well-being.

Fortunately there is an antidote for the virus of hypocrisy. The antidote is a spiritually healthy church devoted to both grace and truth. Such a church nurtures sincere faith and deals with sin honestly and redemptively. Healthy churches guard authentic faith by practicing several disciplines in the power of the Holy Spirit:

1. Healthy churches **pursue God's holiness from the inside out.**

2. Healthy churches **address sin with honesty and grace.**

3. Healthy churches **speak the truth in love as a way of life.**

4. Healthy churches **fear the Lord.**

Hundreds of churches around the world lack spiritual health and power. Unlike the Jerusalem church, they have left hidden sins unaddressed and have settled for the appearance of godliness. What a tragedy. Isn't it time for us to nurture sincere and authentic faith by building healthy churches committed to grace and truth?

Day One

Healthy churches pursue God's holiness from the inside out

³²All the believers were one in heart and mind. No one claimed that any of his possessions was his own, but they shared everything they had. ³³With great power the apostles continued to testify to the resurrection of the Lord Jesus, and much grace was upon them all. ³⁴There were no needy persons among them. For from time to time those who owned lands or houses sold them, brought the money from the sales ³⁵and put it at the apostles' feet, and it was distributed to anyone as he had need.

³⁶Joseph, a Levite from Cyprus, whom the apostles called Barnabas (which means Son of Encouragement), ³⁷sold a field he owned and brought the money and put it at the apostles' feet.   —Acts 4:32-37

¹Now a man named Ananias, together with his wife Sapphira, also sold a piece of property. ²With his wife's full knowledge he kept back part of the money for himself, but brought the rest and put it at the apostles' feet.

³Then Peter said, "Ananias, how is it that Satan has so filled your heart that you have lied to the Holy Spirit and have kept for yourself some of the money you received for the land? ⁴Didn't it belong to you before it was sold? And after it was sold, wasn't the money at your disposal? What made you think of doing such a thing? You have not lied to men but to God."   —Acts 5:1-4

The Bible uses a beautiful word to describe a life that reflects the goodness of God's character. That word is *holy*. It literally means "set apart." It carries the idea of something sacred and noble, as opposed to something common and ordinary. To be holy is to live a life set apart for God's sacred purposes.

Paul used a wonderful illustration to explain the concept of holiness to Timothy. He put it like this:

> *In a large house there are articles not only of gold and silver, but also of wood and clay; some are for noble purposes and some for ignoble. If a man cleanses himself from the latter, he will be an instrument for noble purposes, made holy, useful to the Master and prepared to do any good work* (2 Timothy 2:20-21).

So pursuing God's holiness is the process of growing into our noble identity as people set apart by Christ to enjoy and glorify God. ***How did Peter write about holiness in 1 Peter 1:13-15?*** _____

_____

_____

_____

_____

_____

¹³Therefore, prepare your minds for action; be self-controlled; set your hope fully on the grace to be given you when Jesus Christ is revealed. ¹⁴As obedient children, do not conform to the evil desires you had when you lived in ignorance. ¹⁵But just as he who called you is holy, so be holy in all you do....
—1 Peter 1:13-15

Did you notice how Peter focused on…

- Preparing our minds for action…
- Setting our hope on Christ…
- And not conforming to evil desires?

Holiness begins on the inside with our thoughts, hopes and desires. Becoming holy as God is holy can be seen in our actions, but it begins with our heart motives.

Take a few minutes to compare Barnabas in Acts 4:32-37 with Ananias and Sapphira in Acts 5:1-4. *What was different about their choices and motives?* _____

_____

_____

_____

_____

Why do you think Peter called the actions of Ananias and Sapphira lying to the Holy Spirit and testing the Spirit? _____

_____

_____

_____

Too often we worry about how other Christians see us. It creates a subtle pressure to live our Christian lives for the approval of people instead of for God's pleasure. *What did Jesus teach about this in Matthew 6:1-4?* _____

_____

_____

_____

What is the danger of focusing on external behaviors instead of growing in holiness from the inside out? _____

_____

_____

_____

Finish today's study by brainstorming about how your church can help believers grow in holiness from the inside out. _____

_____

_____

_____

_____

_____

[1]"Be careful not to do your 'acts of righteousness' before men, to be seen by them. If you do, you will have no reward from your Father in heaven.

[2]"So when you give to the needy, do not announce it with trumpets, as the hypocrites do in the synagogues and on the streets, to be honored by men. I tell you the truth, they have received their reward in full. [3]But when you give to the needy, do not let your left hand know what your right hand is doing, [4]so that your giving may be in secret. Then your Father, who sees what is done in secret, will reward you."

—Matthew 6:1-4

Day Two

Healthy churches address sin with honesty and grace

Then Peter said, "Ananias, how is it that Satan has so filled your heart that you have lied to the Holy Spirit…?" (Acts 5:3).

When congregations pursue holiness from the inside out, they nurture the right environment for addressing sin. A spirit of honesty and grace enables us to deal with sin issues openly and gently. I know what you are thinking: There was nothing gentle about the way God dealt with Ananias and Sapphira. We must understand, however, that God acted in a dramatic way to warn his young church against the danger of spiritual dishonesty and hidden sin. It was a teachable moment.

Years ago I accepted a call to become pastor of a congregation that had a history of spiritual leaders who had fallen into moral failure. In each case the church board dealt with the failure behind closed doors in order to save the person and the church from embarrassment. The failed leaders were removed from their positions and left the church without the congregation knowing what had happened. The board members acted out of good intentions, but their unwillingness to address the issues openly created a spirit of distrust in the church. The members of the congregation were left with rumors and unanswered questions.

Within a couple of years of becoming the church's pastor, I had to deal with another instance of leadership failure. This time I led the board to address the matter openly. We were discrete about the specifics, yet we included the congregation in a process of repentance and restoration. As a leadership team, we also asked the congregation's forgiveness for not being more open with them in the past. God honored our attempts to lead with honesty and grace. The congregation's trust in us as leaders grew, and in time the failed leader was restored.

I am not suggesting we should uncover every hidden sin in a public way. I am suggesting it is dangerous to the church's health to leave hidden sins unaddressed.

What does 1 Timothy 5:19-20 teach about addressing the sins of spiritual leaders?

_____

_____

_____

_____

[19]Do not entertain an accusation against an elder unless it is brought by two or three witnesses. [20]Those who sin are to be rebuked publicly, so that the others may take warning.—**1 Timothy 5:19-20**

What does James 5:15-16 teach us about confessing our sins to each other? _____

_____

_____

_____

Often pride prevents us from seeking the help of other Christians when we are struggling with hidden sins. Instead of confessing the matter to a mature and trusted believer, we keep it hidden. We all need brothers and sisters in our lives with whom we can be honest about our struggles. It is liberating when we bring hidden sins into the light.

What does Galatians 6:1-3 teach about how we should help each other escape enslaving sins? _____

_____

_____

_____

_____

Why do you think a spirit of gentleness and humility is so important to the process of restoring those who are ensnared in sin? _____

_____

_____

_____

_____

15And the prayer offered in faith will make the sick person well; the Lord will raise him up. If he has sinned, he will be forgiven. 16Therefore confess your sins to each other and pray for each other so that you may be healed. The prayer of a righteous man is powerful and effective.
—James 5:15-16

1Brothers, if someone is caught in a sin, you who are spiritual should restore him gently. But watch yourself, or you also may be tempted. 2Carry each other's burdens, and in this way you will fulfill the law of Christ. 3If anyone thinks he is something when he is nothing, he deceives himself.
—Galatians 6:1-3

14Then we will no longer be infants, tossed back and forth by the waves, and blown here and there by every wind of teaching and by the cunning and craftiness of men in their deceitful scheming. 15Instead, speaking the truth in love, we will in all things grow up into him who is the Head, that is, Christ. 16From him the whole body, joined and held together by every supporting ligament, grows and builds itself up in love, as each part does its work. —Ephesians 4:14-16

25Therefore each of you must put off falsehood and speak truthfully to his neighbor, for we are all members of one body. 26"In your anger do not sin": Do not let the sun go down while you are still angry, 27and do not give the devil a foothold. 28He who has been stealing must steal no longer, but must work, doing something useful with his own hands, that he may have something to share with those in need.

29Do not let any unwholesome talk come out of your mouths, but only what is helpful for building others up according to their needs, that it may benefit those who listen. 30And do not grieve the Holy Spirit of God, with whom you were sealed for the day of redemption. 31Get rid of all bitterness, rage and anger, brawling and slander, along with every form of malice. 32Be kind and compassionate to one another, forgiving each other, just as in Christ God forgave you.

—Ephesians 4:25-32

Day Three

Healthy churches speak the truth in love

Nurturing a spirit of honesty and grace is essential to becoming a spiritually healthy and empowered church. It goes beyond addressing sin to how we work through our differences and settle our offenses on a daily basis. Too often our churches become like big dysfunctional families. Instead of handling difficult issues directly, honestly and graciously, too often we avoid conflict by stuffing our feelings and then allowing them to leak out in the form of gossip, backbiting or inappropriate expressions of anger.

What did Paul teach in Ephesians 4:14-16 about the importance of speaking the truth in love? _____

_____

_____

_____

Study Ephesians 4:25-32 and list the specific instructions Paul gives about speaking the truth in love:

1. _____
2. _____
3. _____
4. _____
5. _____
6. _____
7. _____
8. _____

Think about the family you grew up in as a child. How did your family handle conflict?

_____

_____

_____

All of us have developed unhealthy habits when it comes to working through differences and offenses with others. *What are your negative tendencies and how do you need to grow in honesty and grace?*_____

_____

_____

_____

What did Jesus teach about how we should work out our offenses with each other?

Matthew 5:23-24 _____

_____

Matthew 7:3-5 _____

_____

Matthew 18:15-17 _____

_____

_____

God struck down Ananias and Sapphiras because he wanted his church to be marked by honesty and sincere faith. We grieve his Spirit when we deal with each other in dishonest and ungracious ways. Conclude today's study by asking God's Spirit to help you and your church to grow in Christ's love and truth.

Day Four

Healthy churches fear the Lord

Great fear seized the whole church and all who heard about these events (Acts 5:11).

What does it mean to fear the Lord? Certainly it means reverence. And it also has the sense of taking God seriously. But is there more to it than merely a general attitude of respect? For the church in Acts 5:1-11, fearing the Lord took on a very specific meaning. *Study the passage again and try to describe what the believers must have felt when Ananias and Sapphira were struck down.* _____

_____

_____

_____

The Lord wanted his church to take sin seriously. He did not want them to take hypocrisy and spiritual deception lightly. It is no small thing to lie to his Spirit and test his Spirit with hidden sins. The Lord was willing to discipline his church in order to correct and protect them. He is willing to do the same today. He loves us too much to abandon us to a sinful path with deadly consequences. Here is what the writer of Hebrews teaches us about our Father's discipline:

23"Therefore, if you are offering your gift at the altar and there remember that your brother has something against you, 24leave your gift there in front of the altar. First go and be reconciled to your brother; then come and offer your gift." —Matthew 5:23-24

3"Why do you look at the speck of sawdust in your brother's eye and pay no attention to the plank in your own eye? 4How can you say to your brother, 'Let me take the speck out of your eye,' when all the time there is a plank in your own eye? 5You hypocrite, first take the plank out of your own eye, and then you will see clearly to remove the speck from your brother's eye." —Matthew 7:3-5

15"If your brother sins against you, go and show him his fault, just between the two of you. If he listens to you, you have won your brother over. 16But if he will not listen, take one or two others along, so that 'every matter may be established by the testimony of two or three witnesses.' 17If he refuses to listen to them, tell it to the church; and if he refuses to listen even to the church, treat him as you would a pagan or a tax collector." —Matthew 18:15-17

4In your struggle against sin, you have not yet resisted to the point of shedding your blood. 5And you have forgotten that word of encouragement that addresses you as sons:

"My son, do not make light of the Lord's discipline,

and do not lose heart when he rebukes you,
6because the Lord disciplines those he loves,
and he punishes everyone he accepts as a son."

7Endure hardship as discipline; God is treating you as sons. For what son is not disciplined by his father? 8If you are not disciplined (and everyone undergoes discipline), then you are illegitimate children and not true sons. 9Moreover, we have all had human fathers who disciplined us and we respected them for it. How much more should we submit to the Father of our spirits and live! 10Our fathers disciplined us for a little while as they thought best; but God disciplines us for our good, that we may share in his holiness. 11No discipline seems pleasant at the time, but painful. Later on, however, it produces a harvest of righteousness and peace for those who have been trained by it.   —Hebrews 12:4-11

Put in your own words what Hebrews 12:4-11 teaches us about the Lord's discipline in our lives. _____

_____

_____

_____

_____

11Great fear seized the whole church and all who heard about these events.

12The apostles performed many miraculous signs and wonders among the people. And all the believers used to meet together in Solomon's Colonnade. 13No one else dared join them, even though they were highly regarded by the people. 14Nevertheless, more and more men and women believed in the Lord and were added to their number. 15As a result, people brought the sick into the streets and laid them on beds and mats so that at least Peter's shadow might fall on some of them as he passed by. 16Crowds gathered also from the towns around Jerusalem, bringing their sick and those tormented by evil spirits, and all of them were healed.   —Acts 5:11-16

Fearing the Lord goes beyond fearing his discipline or even fearing the consequences of sin. My wife Dawn described it like this, "What I fear most is the possibility of losing the joy of my fellowship with Christ." Dawn is right. Jesus said, *"As the Father has loved me, so have I loved you. Now remain in my love. If you obey my commands, you will remain in my love…"* (John 15:9-10).

The Lord doesn't stop loving us when we persist in a disobedient way of life. But we step out of the joy and blessing of his love. We don't remain in a close, loving relationship with him. What do we risk losing?

- The joy of his love.
- The power of his Spirit.
- The effectiveness of our prayers.
- The peace of his presence.
- The fruitfulness of blessing others.
- The ability to help the church grow in spiritual health and power.

Study Acts 5:11-16. What happened as a result of the Jerusalem church fearing the Lord?

_____

_____

_____

_____

_____

As a church, we will not grow in spiritual power and fruitfulness until we come to terms with hidden sins and respond to the Lord in loving and reverent obedience. He is gracious and merciful. His forgiveness is inexhaustible. But so much is at risk when we turn from his loving will. Please don't judge your church or anyone in your church about this matter. Make it about the Lord's dealing in your life. Then pray for your church family.

Day Five

Bringing it home

OK, so God hasn't struck anyone dead in your church lately. Or maybe he has…. Let's not let this study in Acts 5 slip away. Let's bring it home! Reflect on the following questions:

Are there hidden and unaddressed sins in my life that I need to confess to others?

_____

_____

Who can I talk to about this matter that will be gentle, humble and godly? _____

_____

_____

Is there anyone I have hurt or offended? How should I go to him/her? _____

_____

_____

Am I feeling resentment toward anyone who has offended me? How should I go to him/her? _____

_____

How does God want to deal with my heart attitudes, desires and fears to help me grow from the inside out? _____

_____

_____

In what way have I been ungracious or dishonest with people instead of speaking the truth in love? _____

_____

_____

What specifically do I need to begin doing differently in order to grow as a person who speaks the truth in love? _____

_____

_____

What about fearing the Lord? Where do I need to take his commands more seriously? Where am I testing his Spirit? _____

_____

_____

What is our
Guiding Conviction?

Spirit-filled churches nurture and guard faith that springs from sincere hearts.

Here is the guiding conviction: Spirit-filled churches nurture and guard faith that springs from sincere hearts.

Is it possible that you are an Annanias or a Sapphira in the life of your church? Is there a hidden sin or a pattern of ongoing sin in your life that is hindering the Spirit's work in your congregation? The theme of our study is "Fire and Reign." We will not experience the growing reign of Christ in our lives and our churches without the purifying fire of God's Spirit. He desires to do a deep work of conviction, repentance and transformation in our attitudes, affections and behavior. Don't leave this lesson behind without asking the Holy Spirit to search your heart.

Every one of us longs to be the real deal. We want to be a Barnabas who encourages others with an authentic and contagious faith. May we be devoted to becoming the kind of church that nurtures sincere faith.

For Group Discussion

1. Without naming names, tell the group about an incident of hypocrisy you've witnessed in a church.

2. What, specifically, was Ananias' and Sapphira's lie to the Holy Spirit? Do you feel God dealt with them harshly? What was he protecting?

3. Why must holiness always begin its work inside us? How are our thoughts, motives, hopes and desires transformed to those that please Christ? (Day One)

4. Why might church leaders try to deal secretly with sin? When should it become a public matter?

5. If our church wants to address sin with honesty and grace, how well are we doing in this area? (Day Two)

    1------2------3------4------5------6------7------8------9------10
    Ignore sin   Not enough   Healthy balance
    completely   grace or not   of grace
                                  enough truth   and truth

6. Describe a time you have been on the receiving end of someone speaking the truth in love. How did that conversation affect you? (Day Three)

7. How do family conflict patterns affect how churches deal with conflict? Evaluate your ability/inability to "tell the truth about yourself to yourself."

8. What does it mean to "fear the Lord"? How does fear of the Lord show up in our church's life? (Day Four)

PRAYER POINT • First, express to God your desire to live a holy life. Then let's pray that our church fears the Lord in a healthy way. Ask God to give us wisdom to handle sin with both grace and truth.

Lesson Eight

Multiplying His Leaders

In those days when the number of disciples was increasing, the Grecian Jews among them complained against the Hebraic Jews because their widows were being overlooked in the daily distribution of food. 2So the Twelve gathered all the disciples together and said, "It would not be right for us to neglect the ministry of the word of God in order to wait on tables. 3Brothers, choose seven men from among you who are known to be full of the Spirit and wisdom. We will turn this responsibility over to them 4and will give our attention to prayer and the ministry of the word.

5This proposal pleased the whole group. They chose Stephen, a man full of faith and of the Holy Spirit; also Philip, Procorus, Nicanor, Timon, Parmenas, and Nicolas from Antioch, a convert to Judaism. 6They presented these men to the apostles, who prayed and laid their hands on them.

7So the word of God spread. The number of disciples in Jerusalem increased rapidly, and a large number of priests became obedient to the faith.

Acts 6:1-7

I first became a pastor at the age of 26 in Estes Park, Colo. As the church began to grow, I felt increasingly overwhelmed by multiple tasks and responsibilities. I knew we needed a team of leaders to better serve the congregation and reach our community. We had a number of boards and committees, but they didn't multiply my ability to lead. In fact, tending to boards and committees required an increasing amount of my time and energy. So I began to pray, asking the Lord to raise up several leaders to serve alongside me. The Lord gave me Ivan Sandau, John Montgomery and Al Maley. We didn't pay them a dime, but we entrusted them to lead three key ministries in the life of our church. Since those days I have led larger ministries and worked with wonderful staffs, but I have never served with a better leadership team.

Problems always come with growth. The Jerusalem church not only grew in numbers — it grew in diversity and complexity. Luke described a conflict between two groups of believers. Hebraic Jews were those who were born and raised in Judea. The Grecian Jews, however, had returned to Judea after living in various other places around the Roman Empire. Ethnically they were Jewish but culturally they were more Greek in their worldview. They also tended to be more affluent and less provincial than the Hebraic Jews. It is no surprise that misunderstandings and differences would arise between these two cultural groups. In this case, the Grecian Jews felt their widows were being neglected when food was distributed.

The complaint underscored a growing need in the church. The 12 apostles could no longer provide adequate care and leadership for the group's number and diversity of believers. In addition, the apostles found themselves distracted from focusing on prayer and the ministry of the Word. The early church needed to multiply Spirit-filled leaders.

The sixth chapter of Acts gives us a frame of reference for thinking about multiplying leaders. The Jerusalem church needed to expand its leadership base beyond the apostles. So the 12 instructed the congregation, in Acts 6:3, to select leaders *"who are known to be full of the Spirit and wisdom."* The leadership selection process points us to five broad areas of concern. Five "Cs" identify the concerns we use to address developing, selecting and deploying spiritual leaders:

1. CHARACTER

   Trustworthy reputation. The Jerusalem believers were told to select leaders whose reputations were *"known"* by the congregation. The clear implication is that leaders should be marked by trustworthy character — by a good reputation.

2. CHARISMA

   A Spirit-filled life. The apostles also told the church to choose leaders who were *"full of the Spirit."* If the first level of concern is proven "character," then the second level is "charisma" — the evidence of spiritual empowerment.

3. COMPETENCE

   Wise judgment and leadership. The Jerusalem church was also instructed to select leaders who were known to be *"full of wisdom."* Wisdom speaks of leadership that is marked by both knowledge and sound judgment.

4. COMMISSIONED

   Called and empowered. When the Jerusalem church selected seven leaders who were known to be full of the Spirit and wisdom, they presented them to the apostles, who then *"prayed and laid their hands on them."*

5. CONNECTED

   Team leadership. The apostles said, "We will turn this responsibility over to them and will give our attention to prayer and the ministry of the Word." Each leader had a calling to fulfill as they worked together as a team to lead the church.

Spirit-filled churches multiply and empower Spirit-filled leaders.

Day One

Character: a trustworthy reputation

Brothers, choose seven men from among you who are known to be… (Acts 6:3a).

The apostles understood that character is the currency of leadership. The credibility of a trustworthy life is essential. Paul would later emphasize this concern in his instructions to Timothy and Titus regarding the qualifications for elders and deacons. He used phrases like "above reproach," "blameless," "not a recent convert," "worthy of respect," "a good reputation with outsiders" and "they must first be tested." It was this issue of proven character that Paul had in mind when he encouraged young Timothy to *"set an example for the believers in speech, in life, in love, in faith and in purity"* (1 Timothy 4:12).

Study the nature of the conflict in Acts 6:1. ***Why was it necessary for the selected leaders to be trusted by both the Hebraic and the Grecian Jews?*** _____

_____

_____

Gary McIntosh and Sam Rima, in their book *Overcoming the Dark Side of Leadership*, identify a number of negative life patterns that undermine the effectiveness of leaders. They write about leaders who are compulsive, narcissistic, paranoid, codependent or passive-aggressive. Every leader struggles with dark-side issues of various kinds: patterns of anger, lust, selfish ambition, greed, substance abuse, impulsive decision making, fear, procrastination, people-pleasing, prejudice, tendencies to control and manipulate people — and the list goes on. Every leader must address any personal issue that may sabotage his or her leadership effectiveness.

Not all of us will be called to serve in official leadership roles, but all of us lead in one way or another.

Study the qualifications for leaders listed in 1 Timothy 3:1-13. Invite the Lord to examine your heart. Then identify several character traits the Lord is developing in your life and several areas that need to be addressed:

CHARACTER TRAITS: areas of growing maturity	DARK-SIDE ISSUES: life patterns undermining effectiveness

1Here is a trustworthy saying: If anyone sets his heart on being an overseer, he desires a noble task. 2Now the overseer must be above reproach, the husband of but one wife, temperate, self-controlled, respectable, hospitable, able to teach, 3not given to drunkenness, not violent but gentle, not quarrelsome, not a lover of money. 4He must manage his own family well and see that his children obey him with proper respect. 5(If anyone does not know how to manage his own family, how can he take care of God's church?) 6He must not be a recent convert, or he may become conceited and fall under the same judgment as the devil. 7He must also have a good reputation with outsiders, so that he will not fall into disgrace and into the devil's trap.

8Deacons, likewise, are to be men worthy of respect, sincere, not indulging in much wine, and not pursuing dishonest gain. 9They must keep hold of the deep truths of the faith with a clear conscience. 10They must first be tested; and then if there is nothing against them, let them serve as deacons.

11In the same way, their wives are to be women worthy of respect, not malicious talkers but temperate and trustworthy in everything.

12A deacon must be the husband of but one wife and must manage his children and his household well. 13Those who have served well gain an excellent standing and great assurance in their faith in Christ Jesus.

—1 Timothy 3:1-13

Now spend a few minutes identifying the one or two character issues you most need to address. _____

_____

_____

_____

Day Two

Charisma: a Spirit-filled life

…who are known to be full of the Spirit… (Acts 6:3b).

Charisma is the Greek word the New Testament uses to speak of spiritual gifts. Both the gifts of the Spirit and the fruit of the Spirit are abundantly evident in a leader who is full of the Spirit. When Jesus prepared his original disciples, he majored on helping them live and minister in the power of the Spirit. Paul reminded Timothy to *"fan into flame the gift of God, which is in you…"* (2 Timothy 1:6).

Stephen was one of the seven spiritual leaders the congregation selected. **Read Acts 6:5, 8-10 and describe the spiritual gifts and graces you see in his life.** _____

_____

_____

_____

Now picture a leader in your church you would call "full of the Spirit." **What is it about that person's life that evidences the power of the Holy Spirit?** _____

_____

_____

_____

> They chose Stephen, a man full of faith and of the Holy Spirit.…   —**Acts 6:5**
>
> 8Now Stephen, a man full of God's grace and power, did great wonders and miraculous signs among the people. 9Opposition arose, however, from members of the Synagogue of the Freedmen (as it was called) — Jews of Cyrene and Alexandria as well as the provinces of Cilicia and Asia. These men began to argue with Stephen, 10but they could not stand up against his wisdom or the Spirit by whom he spoke.
> —**Acts 6:8-10**

There are three reasons why we need to have a grasp of how the Holy Spirit is uniquely empowering our lives:

- First, it will help each of us lead out of our personal giftedness instead of adopting a leadership style that doesn't fit the way God has designed us. For example, a leader with a dominant gift of mercy will exercise influence in a very different way from someone with a strong gift of administration.

- Second, it will help us develop leadership teams made up of people who bring the balance and synergy of multiple gifts and graces. One leader's "flat-sides" will be rounded out by another leader's strengths.

- In addition, it will enable leaders to maximize their gifts and grow in grace as they seek the Spirit's empowerment.

Study the examples of spiritual gifts listed in Romans 12:6-8. Also study the Fruit of the Spirit in Galatians 5:22-23. You may want to ask others for input and feedback as you respond to the following questions:

SPIRITUAL GIFTS AND GRACES: How is the Holy Spirit empowering my life and ministry?	AREAS OF IMBALANCE: In what areas do I need team members to complement my gifts, and in what areas do I need a fresh work of God's Spirit?

Why do you think we often try to exercise leadership or attempt ministry out of our own abilities instead of relying on the Holy Spirit's power? _____

_____

_____

_____

Conclude today's study by thanking the Holy Spirit for his work in your life. Write a brief prayer of thanksgiving. _____

_____

_____

_____

_____

6We have different gifts, according to the grace given us. If a man's gift is prophesying, let him use it in proportion to his faith. 7If it is serving, let him serve; if it is teaching, let him teach; 8if it is encouraging, let him encourage; if it is contributing to the needs of others, let him give generously; if it is leadership, let him govern diligently; if it is showing mercy, let him do it cheerfully.
 –Romans 12:6-8

22But the fruit of the Spirit is love, joy, peace, patience, kindness, goodness, faithfulness, 23gentleness and self-control. Against such things there is no law.
 –Galatians 5:22-23

Day Three

Competence: wise judgment and leadership

…who are known to be full of the Spirit and wisdom… (Acts 6:3b).

Wisdom is the skillful application of knowledge. Competent leaders demonstrate sound judgment. They are purposeful, thoughtful and prudent, as opposed to those who are rash, impulsive and reactionary. They lead out of sound doctrine and biblical convictions. Paul taught that one test of wisdom is how we manage our closest relationships at home.

Leading with wisdom requires the application of learned skills and expertise in matters both theological and commonplace. Spiritual leadership is not only a matter of character and charisma — it is also a matter of competence.

Wisdom, however, goes beyond knowledge, skill and expertise. It has to do with a heart that is sensitive to God's priorities. The apostle James put it like this, *"The wisdom that comes from heaven is first of all pure; then peace-loving, considerate, submissive, full of mercy and good fruit, impartial and sincere"* (James 3:17). A leader may be competent at business yet incompetent at God's business. Wisdom requires leaders to find answers to two equally important questions:

- What knowledge and skills do we need to gain in order to lead the congregation toward greater health and fruitfulness?

- Are we allowing the Lord to purify our heart motives and attitudes so that we might lead with heavenly wisdom?

Read James 3:13-18. *How would you contrast earthly wisdom with heavenly wisdom?*

_____

_____

_____

_____

Every leader needs to keep growing in wisdom, whether leading the church, leading a family or simply influencing others to grow in Christ.

Identify a role you are playing in which God is calling you to exercise influence for him.

_____

_____

_____

_____

13Who is wise and understanding among you? Let him show it by his good life, by deeds done in the humility that comes from wisdom. 14But if you harbor bitter envy and selfish ambition in your hearts, do not boast about it or deny the truth. 15Such "wisdom" does not come down from heaven but is earthly, unspiritual, of the devil. 16For where you have envy and selfish ambition, there you find disorder and every evil practice.

17But the wisdom that comes from heaven is first of all pure; then peace-loving, considerate, submissive, full of mercy and good fruit, impartial and sincere. 18Peacemakers who sow in peace raise a harvest of righteousness.   —James 3:13-18

Use the following exercise to start thinking about the knowledge, skills and expertise needed to lead wisely in whatever setting the Lord has called you to influence others.

COMPETENCE: What attitudes, skills and expertise do I bring to this calling?	LEARNING CURVE: What attitudes and skills do I need to develop and what knowledge do I need to gain?

One of the best ways to grow in wisdom is to be mentored by believers who demonstrate wisdom in the areas we need to grow. *List three growth areas for you and three potential mentors:*

GROWTH AREAS	MENTOR
1.	1.
2.	2.
3.	3.

Think about the kind of spiritual wisdom James wote about. *Jot down a prayer expressing specific ways you need to grow in wisdom.* _____

_____

_____

_____

_____

Day Four

Connected: team leadership

…We will turn this responsibility over to them and we will give our attention to prayer and the ministry of the word (Acts 6:3b-4).

Our fourth area of concern is the importance of connecting leaders to serve as a team. The apostles prescribed a leadership model that is not centered around a single leader's gifts and passions. Rather, a team of leaders take on various responsibilities so each one might give attention to specific ministries. Together they serve the church by supporting and submitting to each other.

The apostle Paul wrote about this team leadership model in Ephesians 4:1-16. Study the passage and reflect on the following questions:

¹As a prisoner for the Lord, then, I urge you to live a life worthy of the calling you have received. ²Be completely humble and gentle; be patient, bearing with one another in love. ³Make every effort to keep the unity of the Spirit through the bond of peace. ⁴There is one body and one Spirit — just as you were called to one hope when you were called — ⁵one Lord, one faith, one baptism; ⁶one God and Father of all, who is over all and through all and in all.

⁷But to each one of us grace has been given as Christ apportioned it. ⁸This is why it says:
"When he ascended on high,
he led captives in his train
and gave gifts to men."
⁹(What does "he ascended" mean except that he also descended to the lower, earthly regions? ¹⁰He who descended is the very one who ascended higher than all the heavens, in order to fill the whole universe.) ¹¹It was he who gave some to be apostles, some to be prophets, some to be evangelists, and some to be pastors and teachers, ¹²to prepare God's people for works of service, so that the body of Christ may be built up ¹³until we all reach unity in the faith and in the knowledge of the Son of God and become mature, attaining to the whole measure of the fullness of Christ.

¹⁴Then we will no longer be infants, tossed back and forth by the waves, and blown here and there by every wind of teaching and by the cunning and craftiness of men in their deceitful scheming. ¹⁵Instead, speaking the truth in love, we will in all things grow up into him who is the Head, that is, Christ. ¹⁶From him the whole body, joined and held together by every supporting ligament, grows and builds itself up in love, as each part does its work.   —**Ephesians 4:1-16**

What attitudes named in verses 1-2 are essential for serving together? _____

_____

_____

What should we "make every effort to keep" if we are going to work together (verses 3-6)?

_____

_____

_____

Why should we value the different spiritual gifts different leaders bring to the church (verses 7-12)? _____

_____

_____

What goal do spiritual leaders work together to accomplish (verse 13)? _____

_____

_____

How do we need to talk to each other in order to grow in maturity (verses 14-15)?

_____

_____

How can each of us do his or her part to build up the body (verse 16)? _____

_____

_____

Don't you love the picture of a team of spiritual leaders using various gifts to equip the members of the church for ministry? This is what a healthy, growing church looks like. It is a body building up itself in love.

What steps can leadership teams take to spiritually prepare for the challenge of leading a congregation to spiritual vitality? Here are a few suggestions:

1. Make spiritual and relational vitality the highest priority of your leadership team. Seek the Spirit's help to model the kind of community you want the whole church to become.

2. Develop a growth path. Prayerfully form a process for growth that answers several questions:
   - What spiritual disciplines and accountability do we need to keep growing in character and maturity?
   - What steps are needed to experience a greater work of the Spirit through our leadership team?
   - Who are the mentors and what are the resources we need to grow?
   - How can we help each other keep growing as a leadership team?

3. Embark on the journey together. Determine together as a leadership team to become:
   - A worshiping community that places the highest priority on time to worship, pray and study Scripture together.
   - A learning community that seeks opportunities to grow in wisdom as spiritual leaders.
   - A community of disciples that understands its highest calling is to follow Christ and love each other.

How is the Lord prompting you to pray for the leaders of your church as they serve the Lord together? _____

_____

_____

Day Five

Commissioned: called and empowered

They presented these men to the apostles, who prayed and laid their hands on them (Acts 6:6).

It is not enough for the church to develop and select spiritual leaders. Leaders need to be commissioned and empowered to lead. They need a sense of being called and supported by the congregation. Too many churches appoint leaders and then frustrate their attempt to lead through criticism, disrespect and a rebellious spirit.

What do the following passages teach about our responsibility to spiritual leaders?

Philippians 2:29 _____

_____

_____

Hebrews 13:17 _____

_____

_____

1 Timothy 5:17-18 _____

_____

_____

1 Timothy 5:19-20 _____

_____

_____

Stop and reflect on your attitude toward spiritual leaders. *How does the Holy Spirit want to use you to honor, encourage and support the leaders of your church?* _____

_____

_____

---

²⁹Welcome him in the Lord with great joy, and honor men like him....
—**Philippians 2:29**

Obey your leaders and submit to their authority. They keep watch over you as men who must give an account. Obey them so that their work will be a joy, not a burden, for that would be of no advantage to you.
—**Hebrews 13:17**

¹⁷The elders who direct the affairs of the church well are worthy of double honor, especially those whose work is preaching and teaching. ¹⁸For the Scripture says, "Do not muzzle the ox while it is treading out the grain," and "The worker deserves his wages." ¹⁹Do not entertain an accusation against an elder unless it is brought by two or three witnesses. ²⁰Those who sin are to be rebuked publicly, so that the others may take warning.
—**1 Timothy 5:17-20**

As we commission and honor leaders, they are able to serve Christ with a clear sense of call. They are also able to grow in their calling.

Stephen and Phillip were two of the seven leaders selected by the church. We find their stories in Acts 6-8. While both shared the general call of the church, the Holy Spirit led them to fulfill individual and specific callings. Stephen became a mighty apologist and a martyr whose death altered the course of the church. Phillip served as an evangelist and a cross-cultural missionary. A part of personal growth is affirming our sense of call and discerning the specific ways the Lord is leading us to serve him.

Stop and reflect on what the Lord has been doing in your life and what he has been saying to your spirit to prepare you for spiritual leadership. *How is he burdening your heart for specific needs or giving you a passion for certain ministries? How is he leading you to exercise spiritual influence?* _____

_____

_____

_____

_____

_____

_____

A clear sense of being called by God and commissioned by the church enables leaders to serve Christ with courage and commitment. The leaders who were commissioned in Acts 6:6 served the Jerusalem church during a season of terrible persecution. They understood what Jesus meant when he said, *"No one who puts his hand to the plow and looks back is fit for service in the kingdom of God"* (Luke 9:62). It is the same for us. If the Lord has called us to have a part in leading a congregation toward greater health and fruitfulness, we will face opposition and conflict. It comes with the call.

The cost that comes with leadership is eternally worth the price. When the Jerusalem church multiplied leaders, they overcame a huge obstacle to growth and health. *Read Acts 6:7. What three things happened as a result of enlarging their leadership base?*

1. _____

2. _____

3. _____

Here is the guiding conviction: Spirit-filled churches multiply and empower Spirit-filled leaders.

The Jerusalem church followed the pattern set by Christ. Jesus invested his life in 12 followers. He called them, led them, taught them, commissioned them, died for them and then rose from the dead to govern and empower their ministries. He desires to do the same in our churches today. As the head of the church, Christ seeks to shape leaders so that he might use them to shape the body.

So the word of God spread. The number of disciples in Jerusalem increased rapidly, and a large number of priests became obedient to the faith.
—**Acts 6:7**

What is our *Guiding Conviction?*

Spirit-filled churches multiply and empower Spirit-filled leaders.

For Group Discussion

1. Let's speculate: How did the congregation in Acts 6 recognize that the seven leaders they chose were "full of the Holy Spirit and wisdom"?

2. What aspects of character development does a church leader need? (Day One) Explain why these traits are necessary for reaching people and ministering to them.

3. Who in our church exemplifies charisma — living and ministering in the power of the Holy Spirit? (Day Two) Give evidence to support your choice.

4. Competence seems an obvious leadership characteristic. Tell what special competence is needed to lead in a church setting and why it's crucial. (Day Three)

5. Which leaders does our church formally commission? In your own leadership role, do you sense being commissioned by God? By our church? (Day Five)

6. Rate our church's effectiveness in multiplying Spirit-filled leaders who multiply ministry.

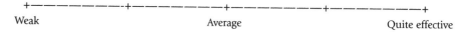

Weak   Average   Quite effective

7. What were the results of the early church appointing Spirit-filled leaders? (Day Five) Identify some implications for our church.

PRAYER POINT • Pray for the leaders of our church. Ask God to multiply the number of our leaders, to better reach our community. For personal reflection: Is God calling you to a new step of involvement in the church?

Lesson Nine

Committed to His Cause

Now Stephen, a man full of God's grace and power, did great wonders and miraculous signs among the people. 9Opposition arose, however, from members of the Synagogue of the Freedmen (as it was called) — Jews of Cyrene and Alexandria as well as the provinces of Cilicia and Asia. These men began to argue with Stephen, 10but they could not stand up against his wisdom or the Spirit by whom he spoke.

11Then they secretly persuaded some men to say, "We have heard Stephen speak words of blasphemy against Moses and against God."

12So they stirred up the people and the elders and the teachers of the law. They seized Stephen and brought him before the Sanhedrin. 13They produced false witnesses, who testified, "This fellow never stops speaking against this holy place and against the law. 14For we have heard him say that this Jesus of Nazareth will destroy this place and change the customs Moses handed down to us."

15All who were sitting in the Sanhedrin looked intently at Stephen, and they saw that his face was like the face of an angel.

Acts 6:8-15

The story of the Jerusalem church culminates in the story of Stephen. He is the exclamation point, the resounding amen, the come-to-Jesus altar call. After Stephen, Luke shifts his focus from Jerusalem to the world beyond. It is Stephen's life and death that changes the course of the early church from a regional phenomenon to a global movement.

Stephen's example illustrates the power of a life fully committed to Christ. Stephen was a man whose life demanded a response from all who met him. Remaining neutral

about Jesus was not an option for those who encountered him. They were forced to make a decision about Stephen and the Lord he served.

- His leadership blessed and inspired the church.
- His ministry impacted the community with God's grace and power.
- His wisdom humbled his opponents.
- His peace astonished his accusers.
- His message infuriated his listeners.
- His death haunted Saul the persecutor, who later became Paul the apostle.
- His martyrdom scattered the church and filled the world with Christ's gospel.

Many of us have been blessed to know Christ-followers like Stephen. We have felt the influence of their wholehearted commitment to Christ. Christians like Stephen are not always easy to be around. They shake our comfortable worlds and challenge our spiritual indifference. Their examples compel us to do something about Jesus and his claims on our lives.

Jim Elliot was such a man. He was a Stephen for my parent's generation. He too was martyred for the cause of Christ. The story of Jim Elliot's death at the hands of Auca tribal warriors inspired thousands around the world to serve Christ. As a young man, Elliot wrote in his journal about his desire to be a "crisis man" — to be a signpost pointing everyone he met to Christ.

Now is as good a time as any to pray a prayer like that of Jim Elliot's — to ask the Lord to make us crisis men and crisis women. Why would we want to slip through life without leaving a ripple when Christ is willing to use us to make a Stephen-like impact on others?

Luke dwells on the story of Stephen as if he were saying, "Stop and see, this is what a Spirit-filled life looks like." Three times Luke used the world "full" to describe Stephen. Here was a man fully committed to Christ and fully submitted to his Spirit. He modeled four Spirit-filled commitments to Christ and his cause.

1. The commitment to live a faith-filled life.
2. The commitment to God-filled ministry.
3. The commitment to wisdom-filled words.
4. The commitment to hope-filled endurance.

One of the most striking features of Stephen's story is his vision of Jesus standing at the right hand of God. Stephen's life and death were filled with the vision of a reigning Christ. Talk about "fire and reign" — God's Spirit flamed in Stephen so that everywhere he went the reign of King Jesus advanced.

> Christ is calling us to lives fully committed to his cause and fully submitted to his Spirit.

Day One

Committed to a faith-filled life

They chose Stephen, a man full of faith and of the Holy Spirit… (Acts 6:5).

When the church was looking for godly leaders to serve alongside the apostles, Stephen was the first person they chose. What did they see in his life? A man full of faith and the Holy Spirit.

I wish I knew more about Stephen. We know his name, *Stephanos*, is Greek, not Hebrew. So he was most likely a Grecian Jew who had returned to live in Jerusalem. I wonder about his early life. Where was he born and raised? What was his occupation? Did he have a wife and children? What brought him back to Jerusalem? How did he come to faith in Christ? Luke did not provide us with any of these personal details about Stephen's life. He simply described his reputation among those who knew him in the early church.

I wonder how you or I would be described by the people in our congregations? If they were to sum up our reputations in one sentence, what might they say about you or about me? Wouldn't we love to be described like Stephen, as people full of faith and full of the Holy Spirit?

The first thing we learn about Stephen is that he was a blessing to the church. He was trusted by his fellow disciples. They looked to him for leadership. He assisted the apostles as a servant-leader, tending to the needs of people and a variety of ministry tasks. More important, he blessed the church with his Spirit-filled faith. It marked everything he did.

When I was a young pastor, God often encouraged me through the faith of one of our deacons. His name was Paul Farrel. Paul possessed a great confidence in God's power and faithfulness. It was often Paul who called our little church to step out in faith when we were struggling over financial decisions or other difficult issues.

A few years ago I had the privilege of speaking at the memorial service for Paul's wife, Florence. She had passed away after a lengthy bout with Alzheimer's. Following the service I knelt beside Paul and thanked him for how his faith had encouraged me during my time as his pastor years ago. He began to weep as we talked about that season in our lives when we served the Lord together as a part of a church trying to follow Christ by faith.

Take a moment to think about individuals who have blessed your church with Spirit-filled faith. Why are they so important to the church? _____

_____

_____

11Then they secretly persuaded some men to say, "We have heard Stephen speak words of blasphemy against Moses and against God."

12So they stirred up the people and the elders and the teachers of the law. They seized Stephen and brought him before the Sanhedrin. 13They produced false witnesses, who testified, "This fellow never stops speaking against this holy place and against the law. 14For we have heard him say that this Jesus of Nazareth will destroy this place and change the customs Moses handed down to us."

15All who were sitting in the Sanhedrin looked intently at Stephen, and they saw that his face was like the face of an angel.—**Acts 6:11-15**

32And what more shall I say? I do not have time to tell about Gideon, Barak, Samson, Jephthah, David, Samuel and the prophets, 33who through faith conquered kingdoms, administered justice, and gained what was promised; who shut the mouths of lions, 34quenched the fury of the flames, and escaped the edge of the sword; whose weakness was turned to strength; and who became powerful in battle and routed foreign armies. 35Women received back their dead, raised to life again. Others were tortured and refused to be released, so that they might gain a better resurrection. 36Some faced jeers and flogging, while still others were chained and put in prison. 37They were stoned; they were sawed in two; they were put to death by the sword. They went about in sheepskins and goatskins, destitute, persecuted and mistreated — 38the world was not worthy of them. They wandered in deserts and mountains, and in caves and holes in the ground.

39These were all commended for their faith, yet none of them received what had been promised. 40God had planned something better for us so that only together with us would they be made perfect.   **—Hebrews 11:32-40**

Study Acts 6:11-15 and describe in your own words how Stephen's faith gave him confidence in the face of false accusations. _____

_____

_____

_____

_____

_____

Hebrews 11 tells the stories of people who lived by faith. Study Hebrews 11:32-40. What point is the writer of Hebrews making about those whose faith is an example for us today?

_____

_____

_____

_____

_____

There will always be those in the church whose works and attitudes will be a source of discouragement and doubt. We don't need any more complainers, critics or cynics. We need a growing number of believers who are committed to living faith-filled lives.

Picture yourself as a faith-filled follower of Christ. How would faith fill...

Your words? _____

_____

_____

Your prayers? _____

_____

_____

Your attitude toward life's trials? _____

_____

_____

Your witness to people who need Christ? _____

_____

_____

Close today's study by writing a prayer of commitment. Ask God's Spirit to fill you with greater faith. _____

_____

_____

_____

_____

Day Two

Committed to God-filled ministry

Now Stephen, a man full of God's grace and power, did great wonders and miraculous signs among the people (Acts 6:8).

God worked in miraculous ways through Stephen's ministry. Signs and wonders demonstrated that his message was from God. Luke tells us Stephen was full of God's grace and power.

In the days of the early church, God often used signs and wonders to verify the message of Christ and to establish the church. We find miracles described on nearly every page

⁴There are different kinds of gifts, but the same Spirit. ⁵There are different kinds of service, but the same Lord. ⁶There are different kinds of working, but the same God works all of them in all men.
— 1 Corinthians 12:4-6

³For by the grace given me I say to every one of you: Do not think of yourself more highly than you ought, but rather think of yourself with sober judgment, in accordance with the measure of faith God has given you. ⁴Just as each of us has one body with many members, and these members do not all have the same function, ⁵so in Christ we who are many form one body, and each member belongs to all the others. ⁶We have different gifts, according to the grace given us. If a man's gift is prophesying, let him use it in proportion to his faith. ⁷If it is serving, let him serve; if it is teaching, let him teach....
— Romans 12:3-7

¹When I came to you, brothers, I did not come with eloquence or superior wisdom as I proclaimed to you the testimony about God. ²For I resolved to know nothing while I was with you except Jesus Christ and him crucified. ³I came to you in weakness and fear, and with much trembling. ⁴My message and my preaching were not with wise and persuasive words, but with a demonstration of the Spirit's power, ⁵so that your faith might not rest on men's wisdom, but on God's power.
— 1 Corinthians 2:1-5

of the Book of Acts. Some suggest it was a special and unique season meant only for the apostolic age. Others teach that signs and wonders should be a normal experience for the church today. When you study the Bible, you discover that God sovereignly determined when to act miraculously to accomplish his purposes. The early church age was one of those times and places that fit his plans and purposes. Our part is to pray and to rely on him. His part is to work in whatever way he pleases.

You and I may never be used by God to bring about miraculous signs and wonders. God does, however, desire to fill our ministries with his grace and power. He wants to work through each of us in powerful ways.

What is being taught in 1 Corinthians 12:4-6 about how God works in different ways through our ministries? _____

_____

_____

_____

_____

_____

Read Romans 12:3-7 and explain what Paul teaches about using the spiritual gifts God gives to each of us. _____

_____

_____

_____

_____

The apostle Paul talked about his desire to serve Christ in the power of God's Spirit. *Study 1 Corinthians 2:1-5 and put in your own words how Paul wanted to minister to the Corinthian church.* _____

_____

_____

_____

Those who are committed to Christ's cause are committed to God-filled ministry. They believe God loves to work through people who trust in his grace and power. When we serve people and minister to their needs, we trust God to touch their lives with his loving grace and life-changing power. Like Paul, we may often feel weak and inadequate when we step into ministry situations. Our only confidence is that God will take our weakness and demonstrate his strength.

We began our study in Acts by stating that this is not a day for standing and watching. Each of us has ministries to fulfill and spiritual gifts to use. Stop and reflect for a moment about how God wants to work through your life.

Who is God calling you to serve? _____

_____

_____

How is God using you to strengthen the church? _____

_____

_____

How is he using you to show his loving grace to someone in need? _____

_____

_____

How is God working in a powerful way through a spiritual gift in your life? _____

_____

_____

Often obstacles like pride, self-centeredness, fear or discouragement get in the way of God-filled ministry. *What does the Holy Spirit need to overcome in your life in order to work through you with greater grace and power?* _____

_____

_____

_____

Day Three

Committed to wisdom-filled words

Opposition arose, however, from members of the Synagogue of the Freedmen (as it was called) — Jews of Cyrene and Alexandria as well as the provinces of Cilicia and Asia. These men began to argue with Stephen, but they could not stand up against his wisdom or the Spirit by which he spoke (Acts 6:9-10).

Wisdom is one of the characteristics of a Spirit-filled life. When Stephen was opposed, he responded with wisdom-filled words. His opponents could not stand up against the wisdom the Holy Spirit brought to his words.

Luke reports the opposition arose from a synagogue made up of Jews from Cyrene and Alexandria. They were Grecian Jews who resented the impact of Stephen's ministry. It is likely that some from their own synagogue were putting their faith in Christ. So these Grecian Jews began to argue publicly with Stephen.

Stephen did not react defensively. He simply relied on the Holy Spirit to give him the words to answer their attacks. When they were unable to stand up against his wisdom, Stephen's opponents resorted to stirring up the people with false charges.

Read Acts 6:11-14 and list the accusations they made against Stephen. _____

_____

_____

_____

Stephen answered these charges in Acts 7:2-53. He replied with a powerful message. Stephen's message had two major themes. First, the presence of God is not confined to the land of Israel or any building, such as the temple. He was making the radical point that God's plan culminating in Christ is meant for all people in all places. Second, Stephen described how people have resisted the Holy Spirit from the day of Abraham to the time of Christ.

Take your Bible and turn to Acts 7 and read verses 2-19. *How did God meet Abraham and work in his life and his descendents outside the Promised Land?* _____

_____

_____

_____

11Then they secretly persuaded some men to say, "We have heard Stephen speak words of blasphemy against Moses and against God."

12So they stirred up the people and the elders and the teachers of the law. They seized Stephen and brought him before the Sanhedrin. 13They produced false witnesses, who testified, "This fellow never stops speaking against this holy place and against the law. 14For we have heard him say that this Jesus of Nazareth will destroy this place and change the customs Moses handed down to us."

—Acts 6:11-14

What opposition did Moses face when he delivered the Israelites from the slavery of Egypt? See verses 20-43. _____

_____

_____

_____

What point did Stephen make about the tabernacle and the temple? See verses 44-50.

_____

_____

_____

How did Stephen conclude his message in verses 51-53? _____

_____

_____

_____

As we study Stephen's response to his accusers, we discover several lessons about speaking wisdom-filled words:

1. Wisdom comes from knowing God's Word. Stephen understood the Scriptures. His words were based on the truths of God's Word.

2. Wisdom has its source in the Holy Spirit. Stephen didn't attempt to be clever or outsmart his opponents. He relied on the Spirit to give him words that would honor God.

3. Wisdom is not afraid of opposition. Stephen made it clear there will always be those who resist the Holy Spirit. There is no need to be fearful or defensive. Wisdom-filled people are not intimidated by opposition.

4. Wisdom boldly exalts Jesus Christ. Stephen didn't defend himself. He boldly proclaimed Christ. He confronted his accusers with the reality of their own guilt. They had betrayed and murdered God's Righteous One.

In what ways do you want the Holy Spirit to fill your words with greater wisdom?

_____

_____

_____

_____

Day Four

Committed to hope-filled endurance

But Stephen, full of the Holy Spirit, looked up to heaven and saw the glory of God, and Jesus standing at the right hand of God (Acts 7:55).

Stephen was committed to Christ to the very end. He was faithful in life and fruitful in death. His accusers were furious and gnashed their teeth at him. But Stephen, filled with the Holy Spirit, was given a vision of the glory of God and Jesus standing at the right hand of God.

Read Acts 7:54-60 and describe the scene as if you were reporting the story for the Jerusalem Post. _____

_____

_____

_____

_____

_____

_____

_____

_____

_____

_____

_____

_____

_____

_____

_____

Why do you think the religious leaders were so angry? _____

_____

_____

_____

54When they heard this, they were furious and gnashed their teeth at him. 55But Stephen, full of the Holy Spirit, looked up to heaven and saw the glory of God, and Jesus standing at the right hand of God. 56"Look," he said, "I see heaven open and the Son of Man standing at the right hand of God."

57At this they covered their ears and, yelling at the top of their voices, they all rushed at him, 58dragged him out of the city and began to stone him. Meanwhile, the witnesses laid their clothes at the feet of a young man named Saul.

59While they were stoning him, Stephen prayed, "Lord Jesus, receive my spirit." 60Then he fell on his knees and cried out, "Lord, do not hold this sin against them." When he had said this, he fell asleep.   —Acts 7:54-60

What impact do you think this experience had on Saul? See Acts 7:59, Acts 8:3 and 1 Timothy 1:15-17. _____

_____

_____

_____

Why do you think the Holy Spirit gave Stephen his heavenly vision? _____

_____

_____

_____

If the Holy Spirit were to give you the same vision he gave to Stephen, how do you think it would impact your life? _____

_____

_____

_____

While they were stoning him, Stephen prayed, "Lord Jesus, receive my spirit."—**Acts 7:59**

But Saul began to destroy the church. Going from house to house, he dragged off men and women and put them in prison.   —**Acts 8:3**

15Here is a trustworthy saying that deserves full acceptance: Christ Jesus came into the world to save sinners — of whom I am the worst. 16But for that very reason I was shown mercy so that in me, the worst of sinners, Christ Jesus might display his unlimited patience as an example for those who would believe on him and receive eternal life. 17Now to the King eternal, immortal, invisible, the only God, be honor and glory for ever and ever. Amen. — **1 Timothy 1:15-17**

Recently, one of my staff members shared a firsthand report of a Stephen-like experience. It happened to a pastor in Southeast Asia. Local officials burst into a believer's home, which also served as his church. They began to tear the place apart and beat him for being a pastor. Over the course of the next five hours they beat him, smashing him with rocks, trying everything to end his life.

Later, our staff member asked him, "Were you ever afraid?" His reply: "At first I was. Early on in the beating I had a vision of Jesus, and my fear went away. I have not felt any ongoing pain from the injuries."

This pastor has moved to another village, but his testimony of this incident, his forgiving his tormentors, his healing and his attitude have left a growing mark on the church he once pastored and on those in the village who were aware of what happened.

We may never have an experience like that of this brother in Southeast Asia, but Jesus is the sustaining hope of every one of us who looks forward to seeing him face to face.

It is this eternal hope we have in Jesus Christ that enables us to persevere for the sake of his cause. Like Stephen, we can endure to the end because we know the joy that is set before us. No one modeled hope-filled endurance better than our Lord Jesus.

¹Therefore, since we are surrounded by such a great cloud of witnesses, let us throw off everything that hinders and the sin that so easily entangles, and let us run with perseverance the race marked out for us. ²Let us fix our eyes on Jesus, the author and perfecter of our faith, who for the joy set before him endured the cross, scorning its shame, and sat down at the right hand of the throne of God. ³Consider him who endured such opposition from sinful men, so that you will not grow weary and lose heart.

⁴In your struggle against sin, you have not yet resisted to the point of shedding your blood. ⁵And you have forgotten that word of encouragement that addresses you as sons:

"My son, do not make light of the Lord's discipline, and do not lose heart when he rebukes you....

—Hebrews 12:1-5

⁵⁹While they were stoning him, Stephen prayed, "Lord Jesus, receive my spirit." ⁶⁰Then he fell on his knees and cried out, "Lord, do not hold this sin against them." When he had said this, he fell asleep.   **—Acts 7:59-60**

Study Hebrews 12:1-5 and describe how we are to follow the example of Jesus when he endured the cross for us. _____

_____

_____

_____

Read Acts 7:59-60 and tell how Stephen followed the example of Jesus in his death.

_____

_____

_____

⁷But we have this treasure in jars of clay to show that this all-surpassing power is from God and not from us. ⁸We are hard pressed on every side, but not crushed; perplexed, but not in despair; ⁹persecuted, but not abandoned; struck down, but not destroyed. ¹⁰We always carry around in our body the death of Jesus, so that the life of Jesus may also be revealed in our body. ¹¹For we who are alive are always being given over to death for Jesus' sake, so that his life may be revealed in our mortal body. ¹²So then, death is at work in us, but life is at work in you.

¹³It is written: "I believed; therefore I have spoken." With that same spirit of faith we also believe and therefore speak, ¹⁴because we know that the one who raised the Lord Jesus from the dead will also raise us with Jesus and present us with you in his presence. ¹⁵All this is for your benefit, so that the grace that is reaching more and more people may cause thanksgiving to overflow to the glory of God.

¹⁶Therefore we do not lose heart. Though outwardly we are wasting away, yet inwardly we are being renewed day by day. ¹⁷For our light and momentary troubles are achieving for us an eternal glory that far outweighs them all. ¹⁸So we fix our eyes not on what is seen, but on what is unseen. For what is seen is temporary, but what is unseen is eternal.   **—2 Corinthians 4:7-18**

The apostle Paul wrote about his own commitment to persevere to the end. Read Paul's words in 2 Corinthians 4:7-18. What enabled him not to lose heart? _____

_____

_____

_____

Close today's lesson by subtracting your age from 100. What number did you come up with? ___. Now imagine the Lord chooses to give you that many more years to serve him in this life. It's not likely, but suppose he does. The number of years you have written down may seem either long or short to you — but compared to eternity it is like a brief breath of steam on a cold day. *Write down how you want to commit your remaining years to Christ.* _____

_____

_____

_____

_____

Day Five

Help me find a better word!

We have talked about commitment in this last lesson of our study. I need to tell you I am not crazy about the word *commitment.* It sounds too much like a grit-the-teeth, duty-bound, try-harder call to faithfulness. Help me find a better word! Turn to the first page of this lesson and cross out the "C" word and replace it with one that sounds less dull and dutiful. If we have learned anything from Stephen, it is this: The power to live and die for Jesus comes from being filled with the Holy Spirit. Human resolve and good intentions will not produce a life full of God's grace and power.

So what do we need from the Holy Spirit to make a Stephen-like impact for the cause of Christ?

1. We need the Holy Spirit to fill us with greater faith. We need it individually, and we need it as churches.

    Holy Spirit, I repent of the following attitudes and fears that hinder my faith:

    _____
    _____

    *Holy Spirit, give me great faith in the following ways:*_____

    _____
    _____

2. We need the Holy Spirit to fill our ministries with God's grace and power.

    Holy Spirit, I repent of those things in my life that hold me back from touching others with your grace and power: _____

    _____
    _____

    *Holy Spirit, I want to experience and express your grace and power in the following ways:*_____

    _____
    _____

3. We need the Holy Spirit to fill our words with God's wisdom.

    Holy Spirit, I repent of the following habits of speaking that are foolish and sinful:

    _____
    _____

Holy Spirit, fill my words with your wisdom in the following ways:

_____

_____

4. We need the Holy Spirit to fill our vision with the glory of God and his Son, King Jesus.

   *Holy Spirit, I repent of focusing my eyes on the things of this world in the following ways:*_____

   _____

   _____

   *Holy Spirit, lift my eyes to Jesus so that my heart might be changed in the following ways:*_____

   _____

   _____

As we come to the conclusion of our "Fire & Reign" study, the story of Stephen inspires us as it inspired the members of the Jerusalem church. Jesus stood to receive Stephen as the martyr gave up his life for Christ's kingdom mission. His example pictures what it means to be filled with the fire of God's Spirit for the expanding reign of God's Son.

The great preacher C.H. Spurgeon spoke of Stephen's martyrdom in the following way:

> *Stephen died like a conqueror.* His name was *Stephanos,* or crown, and truly that day he not only received a crown, but he became the crown of the church as her first martyr. *He* was the conqueror, not his enemies. They stoned his body, but his soul had vanquished them. It was not in their power to move him; his quiet look defied their fury. He went home to his God to hear it said, "Servant of God, well done," and in nothing had his foes despoiled him on the way thither. He was more than a conqueror through him that loved him.

Our study began in Acts 1 with Jesus ascending to the right hand of God. We complete the study seeing Jesus standing at God's right hand, welcoming a faithful servant into his presence. From beginning to end, Jesus raised up a Spirit-filled church in Jerusalem so that his reign might spread from life to life to the very ends of the earth. He is calling you and your church to the same purpose. ***Write out your response to Christ's call.***

_____

_____

_____

_____

_____

_____

_____

_____

_____

_____

_____ ___/___/___
(sign your name and indicate the date signed)

What is our
Guiding Conviction?

Christ is calling
us to lives
fully committed
to his cause and
fully submitted
to his Spirit.

For Group Discussion

1. Jerry Sheveland wrote: "Stephen was a man whose life demanded a response from all who met him. Remaining neutral about Jesus was not an option...." Describe someone you have known who made that kind of impact on people.

2. Identify who in our church exemplifies a Spirit-filled faith. Summarize one example of that faith in action. (Day One)

3. If you could live a completely faith-filled life, how would your words be different? Your prayers? Your attitude about life's trials? Your witness? (Day One)

4. Which of the four points on wisdom-filled words comes hardest for you? Explain why. (Day Three)

5. Stephen's life calls us to stand with the faithful or with those who resist God's Spirit. How can we tell the difference?

6. What does it mean to "fix our eyes on the glory to come"? Describe a time when God displayed his glory through someone in your life.

7. If the Holy Spirit granted you the same vision he gave to dying Stephen, how might it impact your life? What empowers the believer's hope and endurance? (Day Four)

8. What are two or three things you would like to ask from the Holy Spirit so you can make a Stephen-like impact on the lives of your church, family and coworkers? (Day Five)

PRAYER POINT • Ask God to help you face the future with the same faith and courage that characterized Stephen's final moments. Tell God your response in this moment of commitment to the cause of Christ.